Berlitz®

Greek

phrase book & dictionary

Berlitz Publishing
New York   London   Singapore

Contacting the Editors

Every effort has been made to provide accurate information in this publication, but changes are inevitable. The publisher cannot be responsible for any resulting loss, inconvenience or injury. We would appreciate it if readers would call our attention to any errors or outdated information. We also welcome your suggestions; if you come across a relevant expression not in our phrase book, please contact us at: **comments@berlitzpublishing.com**

Printed in China

Editor: Zara Sekhavati
Translation: updated by Wordbank
Cover Design: Rebeka Davies
Interior Design: Beverley Speight
Picture Researcher: Beverley Speight
Cover Photos: Shutterstock

Interior Photos: iStockphoto 126, 138, 141, 150; Glyn Genin/APA 62, 67, 90, 100, 103, 134; Greg Gladman/APA 115; Britta Jaschinski/APA 1, 35, 45, 130; Lucy Johnston/APA 164; Richard Nowitz 12, 17, 20, 55, 56, 94, 96; Gregory Wrona/APA 76, 120, 85 Sylvaine Poitau/APA, 88 Rebecca Erol/APA.

Distribution

UK, Ireland and Europe
Apa Publications (UK) Ltd
sales@insightguides.com
United States and Canada
Ingram Publisher Services
ips@ingramcontent.com
Australia and New Zealand
Woodslane
info@woodslane.com.au
Southeast Asia
Apa Publications (SN) Pte
singaporeoffice@insightguides.com

Worldwide
Apa Publications (UK) Ltd
sales@insightguides.com

Special Sales, Content Licensing, and CoPublishing

Discounts available for bulk quantities. We can create special editions, personalized jackets, and corporate imprints. sales@insightguides.com; www.insightguides.biz

Contents

Food & Drink

People

Leisure Time

Special Requirements

In an Emergency

Dictionary

Pronunciation

This section is designed to make you familiar with the sounds of Greek using our simplified phonetic transcription. You'll find the pronunciation of the Greek letters explained below, together with their 'imitated' equivalents. This system is used throughout the phrase book; simply read the pronunciation as if it were English, noting any special rules below.

Stress is important in Greek, as often the meaning of the word changes depending upon which syllable is stressed. In written Greek, stress is indicated by a small mark (´) on the syllable to be stressed. In the Greek phonetic transcription, stress is indicated with an underline.

Over the last 25 years, the Greek language has been greatly simplified, with the number of stress and breathing marks reduced; however, one may still encounter words written with the more elaborate stress marks, mainly in older Greek texts.

Please note that the question mark is indicated by the semi-colon (;) in Greek.

Consonants

Letter	Approximate Pronunciation	Symbol	Example	Pronunciation
β	like v in voice	**v**	βάζο	_vah•zoh_
δ	voiced th, like th in then	**TH**	δεν	_THehn_
ζ	like z in zoo	**z**	ζω	_zoh_
θ	unvoiced th, like th in thing	**th**	θέλω	_theh•loh_
κ	like k in key	**k**	κότα	_koh•tah_
λ	like l in lemon	**l**	λεμόνι	_leh•moh•nee_
μ	like m in man	**m**	μαμά	_mah•mah_
ν	like n in net	**n**	νέο	_neh•oh_
ξ	like x in fox	**ks**	ξένος	_kseh•nohs_
π	like p in pen	**p**	πένα	_peh•nah_

ρ	trilled like a Scottish r	r	ώρα	*oh•rah*
σ	like s in sit	s	σε	*seh*
ς*	like s in slim	s	ήλιος	*ee•liohs*
τ	like t in tea	t	τι	*tee*
φ	like f in fun	f	φως	*fohs*
χ	like ch in Scottish loch	kh	χαρά	*khah•rah*
ψ	like ps in tops	ps	ψάρι	*psah•ree*
γ	like g + h	gh	γάλα	*ghah•lah*
γγ, γκ	like g in go, but in some cases a more nasal ng as in sing	g	γκαρσόν	*gahr•sohn*
μπ	like b in bath, but in some cases more like mp as in lamp	b	μπαρ	*bahr*
ντ	like d in do, but in some cases more like nd as in end	d	ντομάτα	*doh•mah•tah*
τζ	like j in jazz	j	τζατζίκι	*jah•jee•kee*
τσ	like ts in lets	ts	τσάντα	*tsahn•dah*

* This character is used instead of σ, when the latter falls at the end of a word.

Vowels

Letter	Approximate Pronunciation	Symbol	Example	Pronunciation
α	like a in father	ah	μα	*mah*
ε	like e in ten	eh	θέλω	*theh•loh*
η, ι, υ	like ee in keen	ee	πίνω	*pee•noh*
ο, ω	like o in top	oh	πότε	*poh•teh*
αι	like e in ten	eh	μπαίνω	*beh•noh*
οι, ει, υι	like ee in keen	ee	πλοίο	*plee•oh*

Vowel Combinations

Letters	Approximate Pronunciation	Symbol	Example	Pronunciation
αυ	1) when followed by θ, κ, ξ, π, σ, τ, φ, χ, ψ, like af in after	**ahf**	**αυτός**	_ahf•tohs_
	2) in all other cases, like av in avocado	**ahv**	**αύρα**	_ahv•rah_
ευ	1) when followed by θ, κ, ξ, π, σ, τ, φ, χ, ψ, like ef in effect	**ehf**	**λευκός**	_lehf•kohs_
	2) in all other cases, like ev in ever	**ehv**	**νεύρο**	_nehv•roh_
ου	like oo in zoo	**oo**	**ούζο**	_oo•zoh_
για, γεια	like yah in yard	**yah**	**για**	_yah_
γε, γιε	like ye in yet	**yeh**	**γερό**	_yeh•roh_
ειο, γιο	like yo in yogurt	**yoh**	**γιος**	_yohs_
γι, γυ, γη	like yea in yeast	**yee**	**γύρω**	_yee•roh_
ια, οια	like ia in piano	**iah**	**ποια**	_piah_

Greek is a language with a long history. The language has developed over the centuries into the modern Greek spoken today by approximately 11 million people in Greece and Cyprus, as well as Greek-speaking communities within other countries. It is a phonetic language; the sound of each letter does not usually change with its position. The characters may appear confusing at first; don't be put off by this. With a bit of practice most people can read Greek in just a few hours.

Survival

Arrival & Departure

ESSENTIAL

I'm here on vacation [holiday]/business.	**Είμαι εδώ για διακοπές/δουλειά.** _ee•meh eh•THoh yah THiah•koh•pehs/THoo•liah_
I'm going to…	**Θα…** _thah…_
I'm staying at the…Hotel.	**Μένω στο…ξενοδοχείο.** _meh•noh stoh… kseh•noh•THoh•khee•oh_

YOU MAY HEAR…

Το εισιτήριο/διαβατήριό σας, παρακαλώ. _toh ee•see•tee•ree•oh/THee•ah•vah•tee•ree•oh sahs pah•rah•kah•loh_	Your ticket/ passport, please.
Ποιος είναι ο σκοπός του ταξιδιού σας; _piohs ee•neh oh skoh•pohs too tah•ksee•THee•oo sahs_	What's the purpose of your visit?
Πού μένετε; _poo meh•neh•teh_	Where are you staying?
Πόσο καιρό θα μείνετε; _poh•soh keh•roh thah mee•neh•teh_	How long are you staying?
Με ποιον είστε εδώ; _meh piohn ee•steh eh•THoh_	Who are you with?

Border Control

I'm just passing through.	**Απλώς περνώ από εδώ.** _ahp•lohs pehr•noh ah•poh eh•THoh_
I would like to declare…	**Θα ήθελα να δηλώσω…** _thah ee•theh•lah nah THee•loh•soh…_
I have nothing to declare.	**Δεν έχω να δηλώσω τίποτα.** _THehn eh•khoh nah THee•loh•soh tee•poh•tah_

YOU MAY HEAR...

Έχετε τίποτα να δηλώσετε;
eh·kheh·the tee·poh·tah nah THee·loh·seh·teh

Do you have anything to declare?

Πρέπει να πληρώσετε φόρο για αυτό.
preh·pee nah plee·roh·seh·teh foh·roh yah ahf·toh

You must pay duty on this.

Παρακαλώ ανοίξτε αυτή την τσάντα.
pah·rah·kah·loh ah·nee·ksteh ahf·tee teen tsah·ndah

Please open this bag.

YOU MAY SEE...

ΤΕΛΩΝΕΙΟ *teh·loh·nee·oh*	customs
ΑΦΟΡΟΛΟΓΗΤΑ ΕΙΔΗ *ah·foh·roh·loh·yee·tah ee·THee*	duty-free goods
ΕΙΔΗ ΓΙΑ ΔΗΛΩΣΗ *ee·THee yah THee·loh·see*	goods to declare
ΤΙΠΟΤΑ ΓΙΑ ΔΗΛΩΣΗ *tee·poh·tah yah THee·loh·see*	nothing to declare
ΕΛΕΓΧΟΣ ΔΙΑΒΑΤΗΡΙΩΝ *eh·leh·ghohs THee·ah·vah·tee·ree·ohn*	passport control
ΑΣΤΥΝΟΜΙΑ *ah·stee·noh·mee·ah*	police

Money

ESSENTIAL

Where is...?	**Πού είναι...;** *poo ee·neh...*
the ATM	**το αυτόματο μηχάνημα ανάληψης** *toh ahf·toh·mee·khah·nee·mah ah·nah·lee·psees*
the bank	**η τράπεζα** *ee trah·peh·zah*
the currency exchange office	**γραφείο ανταλλαγής συναλλάγματος** *ghrah·fee·oh ahn·dah·lah·ghees see·nah·lahgh·mah·tohs*
What time does the bank open/close?	**Τι ώρα ανοίγει/κλείνει η τράπεζα;** *tee oh·rah ah·nee·ghee/klee·nee ee trah·peh·zah*
I'd like to change dollars/pounds into euros.	**Θα ήθελα να αλλάξω μερικά δολάρια/λίρες σε ευρώ.** *thah ee·theh·lah nah ah·lah·ksoh meh·ree·kah THoh·lah·ree·ah/meh·ree·kehs lee·rehs seh ehv·roh*
I want to cash some traveler's checks [cheques].	**Θα ήθελα να εξαργυρώσω μερικές ταξιδιωτικές επιταγές.** *thah ee·theh·lah nah eh·ksahr·yee·roh·soh meh·ree·kehs tah·ksee·THee·oh·tee·kehs eh·pee·tah·yehs*

At the Bank

Can I exchange foreign currency/get a cash advance here?	**Μπορώ να αλλάξω συνάλλαγμα εδώ;/να πάρω μετρητά προκαταβολικά εδώ;** *boh·roh nah ah·lah·ksoh see·nah·lahgh·mah eh·THoh/ nah pah·roh meh·tree·tah proh·kah·tah·voh·lee kah eh·THoh*
What's the exchange rate?	**Ποια είναι η τιμή συναλλάγματος;** *piah ee·neh ee tee·mee see·nah·lahgh·mah·tohs*

How much is the fee?	**Πόση προμήθεια χρεώνετε;** _poh·see proh·mee·thee·ah khreh·oh·neh·teh_
I think there's a mistake.	**Νομίζω έγινε λάθος.** _noh·mee·zoh eh·ghee·neh lah·thohs_
I've lost my traveler's checks.	**Έχασα τις ταξιδιωτικές επιταγές μου.** _eh·khah·sah tees tah·ksee·THee·oh·tee·kehseh·pee·tah·yehs moo_
My card was lost.	**Χάθηκε η κάρτα μου.** _khah·thee·keh ee kahr·tah moo_
My credit cards have been stolen.	**Μου έκλεψαν τις πιστωτικές μου κάρτες.** _Moo ehk·leh·psahn tees pees·toh·tee·kehs moo kahr·tehs_
My card doesn't work.	**Η κάρτα μου δεν λειτουργεί.** _ee kahr·tah moo THehn lee·toor·ghee_
The ATM ate my card.	**Το ΑΤΜ κράτησε την κάρτα μου.** _toh ATM krah·tee·seh teen kahr·tah moo_

For Numbers, see page 156.

YOU MAY SEE...

ΕΙΣΑΓΕΤΕ ΤΗΝ ΚΑΡΤΑ _ee·sah·yeh·teh teen kahr·tah_	insert card
ΑΚΥΡΩΣΗ _ah·kee·roh·see_	cancel
ΔΙΑΓΡΑΦΗ _THee·ahgh·rah·fee_	clear
ΕΙΣΑΓΕΤΕ _ee·sah·yeh·teh_	enter
PIN _peen_	PIN
ΑΝΑΛΗΨΗ _ah·nah·lee·psee_	withdraw
ΑΠΟ ΛΟΓΑΡΙΑΣΜΟ ΟΨΕΩΣ _ah·poh loh·ghahr·yahz·moh oh·pseh·ohs_	from checking [current] account
ΑΠΟ ΛΟΓΑΡΙΑΣΜΟ ΤΑΜΙΕΥΤΗΡΙΟΥ _ah·poh loh·ghahr·yahz·moh tah·mee·ehf·tee·ree·oo_	from savings account
ΑΠΟΔΕΙΞΗ _ah·poh·THee·ksee_	receipt

17

All major foreign currencies, traveler's checks and Eurocheques are widely accepted at banks and currency exchange offices throughout Greece. In addition, ATMs can be found outside most main banks; these accept VISA, MasterCard, American Express, Eurocard and a variety of other international bank and credit cards.

Banks are generally open Monday through Friday from 7:30 a.m. or 8:00 a.m. to 2:30 p.m. (1:30 p.m. on Friday). Centrally located banks are also open on Saturday. Currency exchange offices usually stay open until late evening.

YOU MAY SEE...

In 2002, the Greek drachma was replaced with the European Union currency, euro, € (**ευρώ** *ehv•roh*), which is divided into 100 cents (**λεπτό** *lehp•toh*).

Coins: 1, 2, 5, 10, 20, 50 **cents**; €1, 2

Notes: €5, 10, 20, 50, 100, 200, 500

Getting Around

ESSENTIAL

How do I get to town?	**Πώς μπορώ να πάω στην πόλη;** *pohs boh•roh nah pah•oh steen poh•lee*
Where's...?	**Πού είναι...;** *poo ee•neh...*
the airport	**το αεροδρόμιο** *toh ah•eh•roh•THroh•mee•oh*
the train [railway] station	**ο σταθμός των τρένων** *oh stahth•mohs ton treh•nohn*
the bus station	**ο σταθμός των λεωφορείων** *oh stahth•mohs tohn leh•oh•foh•ree•ohn*
the metro station	**ο σταθμός του μετρό** *oh stahth•mohs too meh•troh*
How far is it?	**Πόσο απέχει;** *poh•soh ah•peh•khee*
Where can I buy tickets?	**Από πού μπορώ να αγοράσω εισιτήρια;** *ah•poh poo boh•roh nah ah•ghoh•rah•soh ee•see•tee•ree•ah*
A one-way/ return-trip ticket.	**Ένα απλό εισιτήριο/εισιτήριο με επιστροφή** *eh•nah ahp•loh ee•see•tee•ree•oh/ee•sce•tee•ree•oh meh eh•pees•troh•fee*
How much?	**Πόσο;** *poh•soh*
Is there a discount?	**Υπάρχει μειωμένο εισιτήριο;** *ee•pahr•khee mee•oh•meh•noh ee•see•tee•ree•oh*
Which...?	**Ποια...;** *piah...*
gate	**είσοδος** *ee•soh•THohs*
line	**γραμμή** *ghrah•mee*
platform	**πλατφόρμα** *plaht•fohr•mah*
Where can I get a taxi?	**Πού μπορώ να βρω ταξί;** *poo boh•roh nah vroh tah•ksee*
Please take me to this address.	**Παρακαλώ πηγαίνετέ με σε αυτή τη διεύθυνση.** *pah•rah•kah•loh pee•yeh•neh•the meh seh ahf•tee tee THee•ehf•theen•see*

Where can I rent a car?	**Πού μπορώ να νοικιάσω ένα αυτοκίνητο;**
	poo boh•roh nah nee•kee•ah•soh eh•nah ahf•toh•kee•nee•toh
Can I have a map?	**Μπορώ να έχω ένα χάρτη;**
	boh•roh nah eh•khoh eh•nah khahr•tee

Tickets

When's...to Athens?	**Πότε αναχωρεί...για Αθήνα;**
	poh•the ah•nah•khoh•ree...yah ah•thee•nah
the (first) bus	**το (πρώτο) λεωφορείο** *toh (proh•toh) leh•oh•foh•ree•oh*
the (next) flight	**η (επόμενη) πτήση** *ee (eh•poh•meh•nee) ptee•see*
the (last) train	**το (τελευταίο) τρένο** *toh (teh•lehf•teh•oh) treh•noh*
Where can I buy tickets?	**Από πού μπορώ να αγοράσω εισιτήρια;** *ah•poh poo boh•roh nah ah•ghoh•rah•soh ee•see•tee•ree•ah*
One ticket./Two tickets.	**Ένα εισιτήριο./Δύο εισιτήρια.**
	eh•nah ee•see•tee•ree•oh/THee•oh ee•see•tee•ree•ah
For today/tomorrow.	**Για σήμερα/αύριο.** *yah see•meh•rah/ahv•ree•oh*
A first/economy class ticket.	**Ένα πρώτης/οικονομικής θέσης εισιτήριο.** *eh•nah proh•tees/ee•koh•noh•mee•kees theh•sees ee•see•tee•ree•oh*
A...ticket.	**Ένα εισιτήριο....** *eh•nah ee•see•tee•ree•oh*
one-way	**χωρίς επιστροφή** *khoh•rees eh•pee•stroh•fee*
return trip	**με επιστροφή** *meh eh•pee•stroh•fee*
business class	**για θέση business** *yah theh•see business*
How much?	**Πόσο;** *poh•soh*
Is there a discount for...?	**Υπάρχει μειωμένο εισιτήριο για...;** *ee•pahr•khee mee•oh•meh•noh ee•see•tee•ree•oh yah...*
children	**παιδιά** *peh•THyah*
students	**φοιτητές** *fee•tee•tehs*

senior citizens	**ηλικιωμένοι** ee·lee·kee·oh·_meh_·nee
tourists	**τουρίστες** too·_ree_·stehs
The express bus/ express train, please.	**Το λεωφορείο express/ τρένο express, παρακαλώ.** toh leh·oh·foh·_ree_·oh express/ _treh_·noh express, pah·rah·kah·_loh_
The local bus/train, please.	**Το τοπικό λεωφορείο/τρένο, παρακαλώ.** toh toh·pee·_koh_ leh·oh·foh·_ree_·oh/_treh_·noh, pah·rah·kah·_loh_
I have an e-ticket.	**Έχω e-ticket.** _eh_·khoh ee tee·keht
Can I buy a ticket on the bus/train?	**Μπορώ να άγοράσω εισιτήριο στο λεωφορείο/ τρένο;** boh·_roh_ nah ah·ghoh·_rah_·soh ee·see·_tee_·ree·oh stoh leh·oh·foh·_ree_·oh/_treh_·noh
Do I have to stamp the ticket before boarding?	**Πρέπει να σφραγίσω το εισιτήριο πριν ανέβω;** preh·pee nah sfrah·yee·soh toh ee·see·tee·ree·oh preen ah·neh·voh
Can I return on the same ticket?	**Μπορώ να επιστρέψω με το ίδιο εισιτήριο;** boh·_roh_ nah eh·pee·_streh_·pso meh toh ee·THioh _ee_·see·_tee_·ree·oh
I'd like to…my reservation.	**Θα ήθελα να…την κράτησή μου.** Thah _ee_·theh·lah nah… teen _krah_·tee·_see_ moo
cancel	**ακυρώσω** ah·kee·_roh_·soh
change	**αλλάξω** ah·_lah_·ksoh
confirm	**επιβεβαιώσω** eh·pee·veh·veh·_oh_·soh

Plane

Airport Transfer

How much is a taxi to the airport?	**Πόσο κοστίζει το ταξί ως το αεροδρόμιο;** *poh•soh kohs• tee•zee toh tah•ksee ohs toh ah•eh•roh• THroh•mee•oh*
To…Airport, please.	**Στο…αεροδρόμιο, παρακαλώ.** *stoh…ah•eh•roh• THroh•mee•oh pah•rah•kah•loh*
My airline is…	**Πετάω με την εταιρία…** *peh•tah•oh meh teen eh•teh•ree•ah…*
My flight leaves at…	**Η πτήση μου φεύγει στις…** *ee ptee•see moo fehv•ghee stees…*
I'm in a rush.	**Βιάζομαι.** *vee•ah•zoh•meh*
Can you take an alternate route?	**Μπορείτε να πάτε από άλλο δρόμο;** *boh•ree•teh nah pah•teh ah•poh ah•loh THroh•moh*
Can you drive faster/slower?	**Μπορείτε να πάτε *πιο γρήγορα/αργά*;** *boh•ree•teh nah pah•teh pioh ghree•ghoh•rah/ahr•ghah*

Checking In

Where is the check in desk for flight…?	**Πού είναι το γραφείο παράδοσης αποσκευών για την πτήση…;** *poo ee•neh toh ghrah•fee•oh ah•rah•THoh•sees ah•poh•skeh•vohn yah teen tee•see…*
My name is…	**Λέγομαι…** *leh•ghoh•meh…*

YOU MAY HEAR...

Με ποια εταιρία πετάτε; *meh piah eh•teh•ree•ah peh•tah•teh*
What airline are you flying?

Τοπική ή Διεθνή; *toh•pee•kee ee THee•ehth•nee*
Domestic or International?

Σε ποιον τερματικό σταθμό; *seh piohn tehr•mah•tee•koh stahth•moh*
What terminal?

YOU MAY SEE...

ΑΦΙΞΕΙΣ *ah·fee·ksees*	arrivals
ΑΝΑΧΩΡΗΣΕΙΣ *ah·nah·khoh·ree·sees*	departures
ΠΑΡΑΛΑΒΗ ΑΠΟΣΚΕΥΩΝ *pah·rah·lah·vee ah·pohs·keh·vohn*	baggage claim
Ασφάλεια *ah·sfah·lee·ah*	security
ΠΤΗΣΕΙΣ ΕΣΩΤΕΡΙΚΟΥ *ptee·sees eh·soh·teh·ree·koo*	domestic flights
ΠΤΗΣΕΙΣ ΕΞΩΤΕΡΙΚΟΥ *ptee·sees eh·ksoh·teh·ree·koo*	international flights
ΕΛΕΓΧΟΣ ΑΠΟΣΚΕΥΩΝ *eh·legh·khos ah·pos·keh·vohn*	check-in
ΠΥΛΕΣ ΕΠΙΒΙΒΑΣΗΣ *pee·lehs eh·pee·vee·vah·sees*	boarding gates

I'm going to...	**Πηγαίνω...** *pee·gheh·noh...*
I have...	**Έχω...** *eh·khoh*
one suitcase	**μία βαλίτσα** *mee·ah vah·lee·tsah*
two suitcases	**δύο βαλίτσες** *THee·oh vah·lee·tsehs*
one piece of hand luggage	**μία χειραποσκευή** *mee·ah khee·rah·poh·skehv·ee*
How much luggage is allowed?	**Πόσο είναι το επιτρεπόμενο βάρος;** *poh·soh ee·neh toh eh·pee·treh·poh·meh·noh vah·rohs*
Is that pounds or kilos?	**Είναι σε λίβρες ή σε κιλά;** *ee·neh seh lee·vrehs ee seh kee·lah*
Which terminal?	**Σε ποιο τέρμιναλ;** *seh pi·oh teh·rmee·nahl*
Which gate does	**Από ποια έξοδο φεύγει η πτήση...;** *ah·poh*

flight…leave from?	*piah eh•ksoh•THoh <u>fehv</u>•yee ee <u>ptee</u>•see…*
I'd like a window/	**Θα ήθελα μια θέση στο *παράθυρο/ διάδρομο.*** *thah*
an aisle seat.	*ee•theh•lah mee•<u>ah theh</u>•see toh pah•<u>rah</u>•thee•roh/ THee•<u>ah</u>•THroh•moh*
When do we leave/	**Πότε *φεύγουμε/φθάνουμε;*** *poh•the*
arrive?	*fehv•ghoo•meh/fthah•noo•meh*
Is flight…delayed?	**Υπάρχει καθυστέρηση στην πτήση…;**
	e•<u>pahr</u>•khee kah•thee•<u>steh</u>•ree•see steen <u>tee</u>•see…
How late will it be?	**Πόσο θα αργήσει;** *<u>poh</u>•soh thah ahr•<u>ghee</u>•see*

Luggage

Where is/are…?	**Πού είναι…;** *poo <u>ee</u>•neh…*
the luggage carts [trolleys]	**τα καροτσάκια αποσκευών** *tah kah•roh•<u>tsah</u>•kee•ah ah•pohs•keh•<u>vohn</u>*
the luggage lockers	**οι θυρίδες** *ee thee•<u>ree</u>•THehs*
the luggage claim	**η φύλαξη αποσκευών** *ee <u>fee</u>•lah•ksee h•poh•skeh•<u>vohn</u>*
I've lost my luggage.	**Έχασα τις αποσκευές μου.** *<u>eh</u>•khah•sah tees ah•pohs•keh•<u>vehs</u> moo*
My luggage has been stolen.	**Μου έκλεψαν τις αποσκευές.** *Moo ehk•leh•psahi tees ah•pohs•keh•<u>vehs</u>*
My suitcase was damaged.	**Η βαλίτσα μου χάλασε στη μεταφορά** *ee vah•<u>lee</u>•tsah moo khah•lah•seh stee eh•tah•foh•<u>rah</u>*

Finding your Way

Where is/are…?	**Πού είναι…;** *poo <u>ee</u>•neh…*
the currency exchange office	**το γραφείο ανταλλαγής συναλλάγματος** *toh ghrah•<u>fee</u>•oh ahn•dah•lah•<u>ghees</u> ee•nah•<u>lahgh</u>•mah•tohs*
the car hire	**το γραφείο ενοικιάσεως αυτοκινήτων** *toh ghrah•<u>fee</u>•oh eh•nee•kee•<u>ah</u>•seh•ohs ahf•toh•kee•<u>nee</u>•tohn*
the exit	**η έξοδος** *ee <u>eh</u>•ksoh•THohs*
the taxis	**τα ταξί** *tah tah•<u>ksee</u>*

YOU MAY HEAR...

Ο επόμενος! *oh eh•poh•meh•nohs* Next!

Το εισιτήριο/διαβατήριο σας, παρακαλώ. Your ticket/
toh ee•see•tee•ree•oh/THee•ah•vah•tee•ree•oh passport, please.
sahs pah•rah•kah•loh

Πόσες αποσκευές έχετε; *poh•sehs* How much luggage
ah•poh•skeh•vehs eh•kheh•teh do you have?

Έχετε υπέρβαρο. *eh•kheh•teh ee•pehr•vah•roh* You have excess
baggage.

Αυτό είναι πολύ βαρύ/μεγάλο για That's too heavy/
αποσκευή χειρός. *ahf•toh ee•neh poh•lee vah* large for a carry-on
•ree/meh•gha•loh yah ah•pohs•keh•vee khee•rohs [to carry on board].

Φτιάξατε τις βαλίτσες σας μόνος σας Did you pack these
m /μόνη σας f; *ftee•ah•ksah•teh tees vah•* bags yourself?
lee•tses sahsmoh•nohs sahs/moh•nee sahs

Σας έδωσε κανείς να μεταφέρετε κάτι; *sahs* Did anyone give you
eh•THoh•seh kah•nees nah meh•tah•feh•reh•the anything to carry?
kah•tee

Αδειάστε τις τσέπες σας. Empty your pockets.
ah•THiah•steh tees tseh•pehs sahs

Βγάλτε τα παπούτσια σας. Take off your shoes.
vghahl•teh tah pah•poo•tsiah sahs

Τώρα αρχίζει η επιβίβαση για την πτήση... Now boarding flight...
toh•rah ahr•khee•zee ee eh•pee•vee•vah•see
yah teen ptee•see...

Is there...into town?	**Υπάρχει...για την πόλη;** *ee·pahr·khee...yah teen poh·lee*
a bus	**λεωφορείο** *leh·oh·foh·ree·oh*
a train	**τρένο** *treh·noh*
a metro	**μετρό** *meh·troh*

For Asking Directions, see page 34.

Train

How do I get to the (main) train station?	**Πώς πάνε στον (κεντρικό) σιδηροδρομικό σταθμό;** *pohs pah·neh stohn (kehn·dree·koh) see·THee·roh·THroh·mee·koh stahth·moh*
How far is it?	**Πόσο απέχει;** *poh·soh ah·peh·khee*
Where is/are...?	**Πού είναι...;** *poo ee·neh...*
the ticket office	**το γραφείο εισιτηρίων** *toh ghrah·fee·oh ee·see·tee·ree·ohn*
the information desk	**το γραφείο πληροφοριών** *toh ghrah·fee·oh plee·roh· foh·ree·ohn*
the luggage lockers	**οι θυρίδες** *ee thee·ree·THehs*
the platform	**η αποβάθρα** *ee ah·poh·vahth·rah*
Could I have a schedule [timetable]?	**Μπορώ να έχω ένα πρόγραμμα δρομολογίων;** *boh·roh nah eh·khoh eh·nah proh·ghrah·mah THroh·moh·loh·yee·ohn*
How long is the trip?	**Πόση ώρα διαρκεί το ταξίδι;** *poh·see oh·rah THee·ahr·kee toh tah·ksee·THee*
Is it a direct train?	**Είναι απευθείας τρένο;** *ee·neh ah·pehf·thee·ahs treh·noh*
Do I have to change trains?	**Χρειάζεται να αλλάξω τρένο;** *khree·ah·zeh·the nah ah·lah·ksoh treh·noh*
Is the train on time?	**Το τρένο είναι στην ώρα του;** *toh treh·noh ee·neh steen oh·rah too*

YOU MAY SEE...

ΠΡΟΣ ΑΠΟΒΑΘΡΕΣ *prohs ah·poh·vahth·rehs*	to the platforms
ΠΛΗΡΟΦΟΡΙΕΣ *plee·roh·foh·ree·ehs*	information
ΚΡΑΤΗΣΕΙΣ *krah·tee·sees*	reservations
ΑΙΘΟΥΣΑ ΑΝΑΜΟΝΗΣ *eh·thoo·sah ah·nah·moh·nees*	waiting room
ΑΦΙΞΕΙΣ *ah·fee·ksees*	arrivals
ΑΝΑΧΩΡΗΣΕΙΣ *ah·nah· khoh·ree·sees*	departures

Departures

When is the train to...?	**Πότε φεύγει το τρένο για...;** *poh·teh fehv·ghee toh treh·noh yah...*
Is this the right platform for...?	**Είναι αυτή η σωστή αποβάθρα για το τρένο για...;** *ee·neh ahf·tee ee sohs·tee ah·poh·vahth·rah yah toh treh·noh yah...*
Where is platform...?	**Πού είναι η αποβάθρα...;** *poo ee·neh ee ah·poh·vahth·rah...*
Where do I change for...?	**Πού αλλάζω για...;** *poo ah·lah·zoh yah...*

For Tickets, see page 19.

On Board

Can I sit here/open the window?	**Μπορώ να καθίσω εδώ/ ανοίξω το παράθυρο;** *boh·roh nah kah·thee·soh eh·THoh/ ah·nee·ksoh toh pah·rah·thee·roh*
That's my seat.	**Νομίζω αυτή είναι η θέση μου.** *noh·mee·zoh ahf·tee ee·neh ee theh·see moo*
Here's my reservation.	**Να η κράτησή μου.** *nah ee krah·tee·see moo*

The Greek train system is operated by OSE (**ΟΣΕ, Οργανισμός Σιδηροδρόμων Ελλάδος** oh-_seh_, ohr-ghah-neez-_mohs_ see-_THee_-roh-_THroh_-mohn eh-_lah_-THohs). The network is quite limited and, though the journey is scenic, is usually quite slow. The I/C, Intercity (**Υπερταχεία** ee-pehr-tah-_khee_-ah), makes few stops, but is more expensive. Make sure you reserve a seat in advance. All trains have bars and a sleeping car for longer journeys.

Bus

Where's the bus station?	**Πού είναι ο σταθμός λεωφορείων;** poo _ee_-neh oh stahth-_mohs_ leh-oh-foh-_ree_-ohn
How far is it?	**Πόσο απέχει;** _poh_-soh ah-_peh_-khee
How do I get to. . .?	**Πώς πάνε σε. . .;** pohs _pah_-neh seh. . .
Is this the bus to. . .?	**Είναι αυτό το λεωφορείο για. . .;** _ee_-neh ahf-_toh_ toh leh-oh-foh-_ree_-oh yah. . .
Could you tell me when to get off?	**Μπορείτε να μου πείτε πού να κατέβω;** boh-_ree_-teh nah moo _pee_-teh poo nah kah-_teh_-voh
Do I have to change buses?	**Χρειάζεται να αλλάξω λεωφορείο;** khree-_ah_-zeh-teh nah ah-_lah_-ksoh leh-oh-foh-_ree_-oh
Stop here, please!	**Σταματείστε εδώ, παρακαλώ!** stah-mah-_tees_-teh eh-_THoh_ pah-rah-kah-_loh_

YOU MAY SEE. . .

ΣΤΑΣΗ ΛΕΩΦΟΡΕΙΩΝ _stah_-see leh-oh-foh-_ree_-ohn	bus stop
ΕΙΣΟΔΟΣ/ΕΞΟΔΟΣ _ee_-soh-THohs/_eh_-ksoh-THohs	enter/exit
ΑΚΥΡΩΣΤΕ ΤΟ ΕΙΣΙΤΗΡΙΟ ΣΑΣ ah-kee-_roh_-steh toh ee-see-_tee_-ree-oh sahs	validate your ticket

YOU MAY HEAR...

Επιβιβαστείτε! *eh·pee·vee·vahs·tee·teh* — All aboard!

Τα εισιτήριά σας, παρακαλώ. — Tickets, please
tah ee·see·tee·ree·ah sahs pah·rah·kah·loh

Πρέπει να αλλάξετε σε... — You have to change at...
preh·pee nah ah·lah·kseh·teh seh...

Επόμενη στάση... *eh·poh·meh·nee stah·see...* — Next stop...

Metro

Where's the nearest metro station?	**Πού είναι ο κοντινότερος σταθμός του μετρό;** *poo ee·neh oh koh·ndee·noh·teh·rohs stahth·mohs too meh·troh*
Could I have a map of the metro?	**Μπορώ να έχω ένα χάρτη του μετρό;** *boh·roh nah eh·khoh eh·nah khahr·tee too meh·troh*
Which line should I take for...?	**Ποια γραμμή πρέπει να πάρω για...;** *piah ghrah·mee preh·pee nah pah·roh yah...*
Which direction?	**Προς ποια κατεύθυνση;** *prohs piah kah·tehf·theen·see*
Where do I change for...?	**Πού αλλάζω για...;** *poo ah·lah·zoh yah...*

Athens is the only Greek city currently served by a **μετρό** *(meh·troh)*, subway. Before boarding public transportation you need to buy a ticket at the special kiosks or automatic ticketing machines marked **ΕΙΣΙΤΗΡΙΑ** *(ee·see·tee·ree·ah)*. Validate your ticket in the machine, found by the platform, before you get on. In Athens, tickets are valid for 90 minutes and can be used for buses, metro, trolleybuses, trams and part of the suburban railway. Daily, weekly or monthly tickets and reduced fares are available.

It is likely that after your arrival in Athens, you will be heading straight for the port of Piraeus to catch a ferry. The harbor front is lined with ticket agents; ferry prices are fixed. Each agent tends to sell tickets for one company serving a particular route. A window display (usually in Greek and English) will tell you exactly what islands that ferry goes to. Sleeping on the deck is allowed, but make sure to take a sleeping bag and wear warm clothes, even in July!

Once on an island, you may decide to go on an island tour. Several converted fishing boats run daily trips. Note that throwing anything into the sea off a boat deck is an offense in Greece, and you will be fined if caught.

Is this the right train for...?	Είναι αυτό το σωστό τρένο για...;	_ee_·neh ahf·_toh_ toh sohs·_toh_ treh·noh yah...
How many stops to...?	Πόσες στάσεις μέχρι...;	_poh_·sehs _stah_·sees meh·khree
Where are we?	Πού είμαστε;	poo _ee_·mahs·the

Boat & Ferry

When is the ferry to...?	Πότε φεύγει το φέρρυ-μπωτ για...;	_poh_·the _fehv_·ghee toh _feh_·ree boht yah...
Can I take my car onboard?	Μπορώ να επιβιβάσω το αυτοκίνητό μου;	boh·_roh_ nah eh·pee·vee·_vah_·soh toh ahf·toh _kee_·nee·_toh_ moo
What time is the next sailing?	Πότε είναι ο επόμενος απόπλους;	_poh_·teh _ee_·nehoh eh·_poh_·meh·nohs ah·_poh_·ploos
Can I book a seat/cabin?	Μπορώ να κλείσω θέση/καμπίνα;	boh·_roh_ nah _klee_·soh theh·see/kah·bee·nah
How long is the crossing?	Πόσο διαρκεί το πέρασμα;	_poh_·soh THee·ahr·_kee_ toh _peh_·rah·smah
Where are the life jackets?	Πού είναι τα σωσίβια;	poo _ee_·neh tah soh·_see_·vee·ah

YOU MAY SEE...

ΝΑΥΑΓΟΣΩΣΤΙΚΗ ΛΕΜΒΟΣ *nah·vah·ghoh·sohs·tee·kee lehm·vohs*	life boats
ΣΩΣΙΒΙΑ *soh·see·vee·ah*	life jackets

Taxi

Where can I get a taxi?	**Πού μπορώ να βρω ταξί;** *poo boh·roh nah vroh tah·ksee*
Can you send a taxi?	**Μπορείτε να στείλετε ταξί;** *boh·ree·teh nah stee·leh·te tah·ksee*
Do you have the number for a taxi?	**Έχετε το τηλέφωνο για ταξί;** *eh·kheh·teh toh tee·leh·foh·noh yah tah· ksee*
I'd like a taxi now/ for tomorrow at...	**Θα ήθελα ένα ταξί *τώρα/για αύριο* στις...** *thah ee·theh·lah eh·nah tah·ksee toh·rah/yah ahv·ree·oh stees...*
Pick me up at (place/time)...	**Ελάτε να με πάρετε *από/στις*...** *eh·lah·the nah meh pah·reh·teh ah·poh/stees...*
I'm going to...	**Πηγαίνω...** *pee·gheh·noh...*
this address	**σε αυτή τη διεύθυνση** *seh ahf·tee tee THee·ehf·theen·see*
the airport	**στο αεροδρόμιο** *stoh ah·eh·roh·THroh·mee·oh*
the train [railway] station	**στον σιδηροδρομικό σταθμό** *stohn see·THee·roh·THroh·mee·koh stahth·moh*

In Athens, licensed taxis are yellow with a blue stripe. In all major cities, fares are fixed. For longer distances you should agree to a fare before the trip. Tipping is not compulsory, but it is common to round up the amount due.

I'm late.	**Έχω αργήσει.** _eh_·hoh ahr·_ghee_·see
Can you drive faster/slower?	**Μπορείτε να πάτε πιο γρήγορα/αργά;** boh·_ree_·teh nah _pah_·teh pioh _gree_·ghoh·rah/ahr·_ghah_
Stop/Wait here.	**Σταματήστε/Περιμένετε εδώ.** stah·mah·_tee_·steh/ peh·ree·_meh_·neh·teh eh·_THoh_
How much?	**Πόσο;** _poh_·soh
You said it would cost...euros.	**Είπατε ότι θα κόστιζε...ευρώ.** ee·_pah_·the _oh_·tee thah _kohs_·tee·zeh...ehv·_roh_
Keep the change.	**Κρατείστε τα ρέστα.** krah·_tees_·teh tah _rehs_·tah
A receipt, please.	**Μια απόδειξη, παρακαλώ.** miah ah·_poh_·THee·ksee pah·rah·kah·_loh_

YOU MAY HEAR...

Πού μπορώ να; poo boh·_roh_ nah	Where to?
Πού είναι η διεύθυνση; poo _ee_·neh ee THee·_ehf_·theen·see	What's the address?

Bicycle & Motorbike

I'd like to hire...	**θα ήθελα να νοικιάσω...** thah _ee_·theh·lah nah nee·_kiah_·soh...
a bicycle	**ένα ποδήλατο** _eh_·nah poh·_THee_·lah·toh
a moped	**ένα μοτοποδήλατο** _eh_·nah moh·toh·poh·_THee_·lah·toh
a motorbike	**μία μοτοσικλέτα** _mee_·ah moh·toh·see·_kleh_·tah
How much per day/week?	**Πόσο κοστίζει την ημέρα/την εβδομάδα;** _poh_·soh koh·_stee_·zee teen ee·_meh_·rah/tee ehv·THoh·_mah_·THah
Can I have a helmet/lock?	**Μπορώ να έχω ένα κράνος/μία κλειδαριά;** boh·_roh_ nah _eh_·khoh _eh_·nah _krah_·nohs/_mee_·ah klee·THah·_riah_

Car Hire

Where can I hire a car?	**Πού μπορώ να νοικιάσω ένα αυτοκίνητο;** *poo boh·roh nah nee·kiah·soh eh·nah ahf·toh·kee·nee·toh*
I'd like to hire…	**Θα ήθελα να νοικιάσω ένα…** *thah ee·theh·lah nah nee·kiah·soh eh·nah…*
a cheap/small car	**ένα φτηνό/μικρό αυτοκίνητο** *eh·nah ftee·noh/ mee·kroh ahf·toh·kee·nee·toh*
a 2-/4-door car	**δίπορτο/τετράπορτο αυτοκίνητο** *ee·poh·rtoh/ teh·trah·poh·rtoh ahf·toh·kee·nee·toh*
an automatic/ manual car	**αυτόματο αυτοκίνητο/ αυτοκίνητο με συμπλέκτη** *ahf·toh·mah·toh ahf·toh·kee·nee·toh/ahf·toh·kee· nee·toh meh see·bleh·ktee*
a car with air-conditioning	**αυτοκίνητο με κλιματισμό** *ahf·toh·kee·nee·toh meh klee·mah·tee·smoh*

YOU MAY HEAR…

Έχετε διεθνή άδεια οδήγησης; *eh·kheh·the THee·ehth·nee ah·THee·ah oh·THee·ghee·sees*	Do you have an international driver's license?
Μπορώ να δω το διαβατήριό σας, παρακαλώ; *boh·roh nah THoh toh THee·ah·vah·tee·ree·oh sahs pah·rah·kah·loh*	May I see your passport, please?
Θέλετε ασφάλεια; *theh·leh·teh ah·sfah·lee·ah*	Do you want insurance?
Υπάρχει μία προκαταβολή των… *ee·pahr·khee miah proh·kah·tah·voh·lee tohn…*	There is a deposit of…
Παρακαλώ υπογράψτε εδώ. *pah·rah·kah·loh ee·poh·ghrah·psteh eh·THoh*	Please sign here.

a car seat	**παιδικό κάθισμα αυτοκινήτου** *peh·THee·koh kah·thee·smah ahf·toh·kee·nee·too*
How much...?	**Πόσο κάνει...;** *poh·soh kah·nee...*
per day/week	**την ημέρα/ενδομάδα** *teen ee·meh·rah/ehv·THoh·mah·Tllah*
per kilometer	**το χιλιόμετρο** *toh khee·lee·oh·meht·roh*
for unlimited mileage	**για απεριόριστη απόσταση** *yah ah·peh·ree·oh·rees·tee ah·poh·stah·see*
with insurance	**με ασφάλεια** *meh ah·sfah·lee·ah*
Are there any discounts?	**Υπάρχει έκπτωση;** *ee·pahr·khee ehk·ptoh·see*

Fuel Station

Where's the next fuel station, please?	**Πού είναι το επόμενο βενζινάδικο, παρακαλώ;** *poo ee· neh toh eh·poh·meh·noh vehn·zee·nah·THee·koh pah·rah·kah·loh*
Fill it up, please.	**Γεμίστε το, παρακαλώ.** *yeh·mee·steh toh pah·rah·kah·loh*
...liters, please.	**...λίτρα βενζίνη, παρακαλώ.** *...lee·trah vehn·zee· nee pah·rah·kah·loh*
I'll pay in cash/by credit card.	**Θα πληρώσω τοις μετρητοίς/με πιστωτική κάρτα.** *thah plee·roh·soh tees meh·tree·tees/meh pee·stoh·tee· kee kah·rtah*

YOU MAY SEE...

ΑΠΛΗ *ah·plee*	regular
ΣΟΥΠΕΡ *soo·pehr*	premium [super]
ΝΤΗΖΕΛ *dee·zehl*	diesel

YOU MAY SEE...

 ΑΠΑΓΟΡΕΥΕΤΑΙ Η ΕΠΙ ΤΟΠΟΥ ΣΤΡΟΦΗ
ah·pah·ghoh·reh·veh·teh ee eh pee toh·poo stroh·fee

no u-turn

 **ΥΠΟΧΡΕΩΤΙΚΗ ΠΑΡΑΧΩΡΗΣΗ
ΠΡΟΤΕΡΑΙΟΤΗΤΑΣ**
*ee·pohkh·reh·oh·tee·kee pah·rah·khoh·ree·see
proh·teh·reh·oh·tee·tahs*

yield

 ΥΠΟΧΡΕΩΤΙΚΗ ΔΙΑΚΟΠΗ ΠΟΡΕΙΑΣ
*ee·pohkh·reh·oh·tee·kee THee·ah·koh·pee
poh·ree·ahs*

stop

 ΠΕΡΙΟΧΗ ΑΠΑΓΟΡΕΥΣΗΣ ΣΤΑΘΜΕΥΣΗΣ
*peh·ree·oh·khee ah·pah·ghoh·rehf·sees
stahth·mehf·sees*

no parking

 **ΑΠΑΓΟΡΕΥΕΤΑΙ Η ΣΤΑΣΗ ΚΑΙ Η
ΣΤΑΘΜΕΥΣΗ** *ah·pah·ghoh·reh·veh·teh
ee stah·see keh ee stahth·mehf·see*

no stopping

 ΜΟΝΟΔΡΟΜΟΣ
moh·noh·THroh·mohs

one way

Breakdown & Repair

My car broke down/won't start.	**Το αυτοκίνητό μου χάλασε/δεν παίρνει μπρος.** *toh ahf·toh·kee·nee·toh moo khah·lah·seh/THehn pehr·nee brohs*
Can you fix it today?	**Μπορείτε να το επισκευάσετε σήμερα;** *boh·ree·teh nah toh eh·pees·keh·vah·seh·the see·meh·rah*

When will it be ready?	**Πότε θα είναι έτοιμο;** _poh_·teh thah _ee_·neh _eh_·tee·moh
How much?	**Πόσο;** _poh_·soh
I have a puncture/ flat tyre (tire)	**Έχω σκασμένο λάστιχο** _eh_·khoh skah· _zmeh_·noh _lah_·stee·khoh

Accidents

| There's been an accident. | **Έγινε ένα ατύχημα.** _eh_·yee·neh _eh_·nah ah·_tee_·khee·mah |
| Call an ambulance/ the police. | **Καλέστε** _ένα ασθενοφόρο/την αστυνομία._ kah·_lehs_·teh _eh_·nah ahs·theh·noh·_foh_·roh/teen ahs·tee·noh·_mee_·ah |

Places to Stay

ESSENTIAL

Can you recommend a hotel?	**Μπορείτε να μου συστήσετε ένα ξενοδοχείο;** boh·_ree_·teh nah moo sees·_tee_·seh·teh _eh_·nah kseh·noh·THoh·_khee_·oh
I have a reservation.	**Έχω κλείσει δωμάτιο.** _eh_·khoh _klee_·see THoh·_mah_·tee·oh
My name is...	**Λέγομαι...** _leh_·ghoh·meh...
Do you have a room...?	**Έχετε ελεύθερο δωμάτιο...;** _eh_·kheh·the eh·_lehf_·theh·roh THoh·_mah_·tee·oh...
for one/two	**μονόκλινο/δίκλινο** moh·_noh_·klee·noh/_THee_·klee·noh
with a bathroom	**με μπάνιο** meh _bah_·nioh
with air-conditioning	**με κλιματισμό** meh klee·mah·teez·_moh_
For tonight.	**Γι' απόψε.** yah·_poh_·pseh
For two nights.	**Για δύο βράδια.** yah _THee_·oh vrah·_THee_·ah
For one week.	**Για μια εβδομάδα.** yah _mee_·ah ev·THoh·_mah_·THah

How much?	**Πόσο;** *poh·soh*
Do you have anything cheaper?	**Έχετε τίποτα φθηνότερο;** *eh·kheh·the tee·poh·tah fthee·noh·teh·roh*
When's check-out?	**Τι ώρα πρέπει να αδειάσουμε το δωμάτιο;** *tee oh·rah preh·pee nah ah·THee·ah·soo·meh toh THoh·mah·tee·oh*
Can I leave this in the safe?	**Μπορώ να αφήσω αυτό στη θυρίδα;** *boh·roh nah ah·fee·soh ahf·toh stee thee·ree·THah*
Could we leave our baggage here until…?	**Μπορούμε να αφήσουμε τα πράγματά μας εδώ ως τις…;** *boh·roo·meh nah ah·fee·soo·meh tah prahgh·mah·tah mahs eh·THoh ohs tees…*
Could I have the bill/a receipt?	**Μπορώ να έχω τον λογαριασμό/μιααπόδειξη;** *boh·roh nah eh·hoh tohn loh·ghahr·yahs·moh/miah ah·poh·THee·ksee*
I'll pay in cash/by credit card.	**Θα πληρώσω τοις μετρητοίς/με πιστωτική κάρτα.** *thah plee·roh·soh tees meht·ree·tees/meh pees·toh·tee·kee kahr·tah*

Somewhere to Stay

Can you recommend a hotel?	**Μπορείτε να μου συστήσετε ένα ξενοδοχείο…;** *boh·ree·teh nah moo sees·tee·seh·teh eh·nah kseh·noh·THoh·khee·oh…*
Can you recommend…?	**Μπορείτε να προτείνετε…;** *boh·ree·teh nah proh·tee·neh·teh*
a hostel	**ένα ξενώνα** *eh·nah kseh·noh·nah*
a campsite	**ένα μέρος για κάμπινγκ;** *eh·nah meh·rohs yah kahm·peeng*
a bed and breakfast	**ένα δωμάτιο με πρωινό** *eh·nah THoh·mah·tee·oh meh proh·ee·noh*
What is it near?	**Πού κοντά είναι;** *poo kohn·dah ee·neh*
How do I get there?	**Πώς πάω εκεί;** *pohs pah·oh eh·kee*

At the Hotel

I have a reservation.	**Έχω κλείσει δωμάτιο.** _eh_·hoh _klee_·see _THoh_·_mah_·tee·oh
My name is…	**Λέγομαι…** _leh_·ghoh·meh…
Do you have a room…?	**Έχετε δωμάτιο…;** _eh_·kheh·the _THoh_·_mah_·tee·oh…
with a bathroom [toilet]/shower	**με μπάνιο/ντους** meh _bah_·nioh/doo
with air-conditioning	**με κλιματισμό** meh klee·mah·teez·_moh_
that's smoking/non-smoking	**για καπνιστές/μη καπνιστές** yah kahp·nees·_tehs_/mee kahp·nees·_tehs_
For tonight.	**Γι' απόψε.** yah·_poh_·pseh
For two nights.	**Για δύο βράδια.** yah _THee_·oh _vrah_·THiah
For one week.	**Για μία εβδομάδα.** yah _mee_·ah ev·THoh·_mah_·THah
Does the hotel have…?	**Έχει το ξενοδοχείο…;** _eh_·khee toh kseh·noh·THoh·_khee_·oh…
a computer	**υπολογιστή** ee·poh·loh·ghees·_tee_
an elevator [lift]	**ασανσέρ** ah·sahn·_sehr_
(wireless) internet service	**υπηρεσία (ασύρματου) internet** ee·pee·reh·_see_·ah (ah·_seer_·mah·too) een·tehr·_neht_
room service	**υπηρεσία δωματίου** ee·pee·reh·_see_·ah THoh·mah·_tee_·oo
a pool	**πισίνα** pee·_see_·nah
a gym	**γυμναστήριο** gheem·nahs·_tee_·ree·oh

39

If you didn't reserve a place to stay before your trip, visit the local tourist information office for a list of places to stay. Booking ahead is recommended in the high season, from July to the end of August.

Greece offers a large variety of accommodation options:
Ξενοδοχεία *(ksehn•oh•THoh•khee•ah)*, hotels; **Διαμερίσματα**
(THee•ah•meh•reez•mah•tah), furnished apartments; **Δωμάτια**
(THoh•mah•tee•ah) furnished rooms, with or without a private
bath; **Παραδοσιακά δωμάτια** *(pah•rah•THoh•see•ah•kah*
THoh•mah•tee•ah), apartments in traditional but renovated homes;
Ξενώνας νεότητας *(kseh•noh•nahs neh•oh•tee•tahs)*, youth hostels;
Κάμπιγκ *(kahm•peeng)* campsites and more.

I need...	**χρειάζομαι...** *khree•ah•zoh•meh...*
an extra bed	**άλλο ένα κρεβάτι** *ah•loh eh•nah kreh•vah•tee*
a cot	**ένα ράντζο** *eh•nah rahn•joh*
a crib	**ένα παιδικό κρεβάτι** *eh•nah peh•THee•koh kreh•vah•tee*

Price

How much per night/week?	**Πόσο κάνει** *τη βραδιά/την εβδομάδα; poh•soh kah•nee tee vrah•iah/teen ehv•oh•mah•ah*
Does the price include breakfast/ sales tax [VAT]?	**Η τιμή συμπεριλαμβάνει πρωινό/ΦΠΑ;** *ee tee•mee seem•beh•ree•lahm•vah•nee proh•ee•noh/fee•pee•ah*
Are there any discounts?	**Έχει έκπτωση;** *eh•khee ehk•ptoh•see*

Preferences

Can I see the room?	**Μπορώ να δω το δωμάτιο;** *boh•roh nah doh toh THoh•mah•tee•oh*
I'd like a...room.	**Θα ήθελα...δωμάτιο.** *tha ee•theh•lah...THoh•mah•tee•oh*
better	**καλύτερο** *kah•lee•teh•roh*

bigger	**μεγαλύτερο** meh·ghah·lee·teh·roh
cheaper	**πιο φθηνό** pioh fthee·noh
quieter	**πιο ήσυχο** pioh ee·see·khoh
I'll take it.	**Θα το πάρω.** thah toh pah·roh
No, I won't take it.	**Όχι, δεν θα το πάρω.** oh·khee, THen thah toh pah·roh

Questions

Where's...?	**Πού είναι...;** poo ee·neh...
the bar	**το μπαρ** toh bahr
the bathroom	**το μπάνιο** toh bah·nioh
the elevator [lift]	**το ασανσέρ** toh ah·sahn·sehr
Can I have...?	**Μπορώ να έχω...;** boh·roh nah eh·khoh...
a blanket	**μια κουβέρτα** miah koo·vehr·tah
an iron	**ένα σίδερο** eh·nah see·THeh·roh
the room key/	**το κλειδί δωματίου/την κάρτα** toh klee·THee
key card	THoh·mah·tee·oo/teen kahr·tah
a pillow	**ένα μαξιλάρι** eh·nah mah·ksee·lah·ree
soap	**σαπούνι** sah·poo·nee
toilet paper	**χαρτί υγείας** khahr·tee ee·ghee·ahs
a towel	**μια πετσέτα μπάνιου** miah peh·tseh·tah bah·nee·oo

YOU MAY HEAR...

Το διαβατήριό σας/την πιστωτική σας κάρτα, Your passport/
παρακαλώ. toh ee·ah·vah·tee·ree·oh sahs/teen credit card, please.
pees·toh·tee·kee sahs kahr·tah pah·rah·kah·loh

Παρακαλώ συμπληρώστε αυτό το έντυπο. Please fill out this form.
pah·rah·kah·loh seem·blee·rohs·teh ahf·toh toh
ehn·dee·poh

Υπογράψτε εδώ. ee·pohgh·rahp·steh eh·THoh Sign here.

Tipping depends largely on your class of hotel; the higher the class, the more generous the tip. As a guideline, a euro or two per service rendered is recommended in standard hotels.

Checking out

When's check-out?	**Τι ώρα πρέπει να αδειάσουμε το δωμάτιο;** *tee <u>oh</u>• rah <u>preh</u>•pee nah ah•THee•<u>ah</u>•soo•meh toh THoh•<u>mah</u>•tee•oh*
Could we leave our baggage here until...?	**Μπορούμε να αφήσουμε τα πράγματά μας εδώ ως τις...;** *boh•<u>roo</u>•meh nah ah•<u>fee</u>•soomeh tah <u>prahgh</u>•mah•<u>tah</u> mahs eh•<u>THoh</u> ohs tees...*
Can I have an itemized bill/ a receipt?	**Μπορώ να έχω έναν αναλυτικό λογαριασμό/μια απόδειξη;** *boh•<u>roh</u> nah eh•khoh eh•nah nah•nah•lee•tee•<u>koh</u> loh•ghahr•yahz•<u>moh</u>/miah ah•<u>poh</u>•ee•ksee*
I think there's a mistake in this bill.	**Νομίζω ότι έγινε ένα λάθος στο λογαριασμό.** *noh•<u>mee</u>•zoh <u>oh</u>•tee eh•yee•neh eh•nah <u>lah</u>•thohs stoh loh•ghahr•yahz•<u>moh</u>*
I'll pay in cash/by credit card.	**Θα πληρώσω τοις μετρητοίς/με πιστωτική κάρτα.** *thah plee•<u>roh</u>•soh tees meht•ree•<u>tees</u>/meh pees•toh•tee•<u>kee</u> <u>kahr</u>•tah*

Renting

I've reserved an apartment/ a room.	**Έχω κλείσει ένα διαμέρισμα/δωμάτιο.** *<u>eh</u>•hoh <u>klee</u>•see <u>eh</u>•nah ee•ah•<u>meh</u>•rees•mah/oh•<u>mah</u>•tee•oh*
My name is...	**Λέγομαι...** *<u>leh</u>•ghoh•meh...*
Can I have the key/key card?	**Μπορώ να έχω το κλειδί/την κάρτα;** *boh•<u>roh</u> nah <u>eh</u>•hoh toh klee•<u>THee</u>/teen <u>kahr</u>•tah*
Are there...?	**Υπάρχουν...;** *ee•<u>pahr</u>•khoon...*
dishes	**πιάτα** *<u>piah</u>•tah*

pillows	**μαξιλάρια** *mah•ksee•<u>lah</u>•ree•ah*
sheets	**σεντόνια** *sehn•<u>doh</u>•niah*
towels	**πετσέτες** *peh•<u>tseh</u>•tehs*
kitchen utensils	**οικιακά σκεύη** *ee•kee•ah•<u>kah</u> <u>skeh</u>•vee*
When do I put out the bins/recycling?	**Πότε να βγάλω έξω τα σκουπίδια/ την ανακύκλωση;** *<u>poh</u>•teh nah <u>vghah</u>•loh eh•ksoh tah skoo•<u>pee</u>•THiah/ teen ah•nah•kee•kloh•see*
…has broken down.	**…χάλασε.** *…<u>khah</u>•lah•seh*
How does…work?	**Πώς λειτουργεί…;** *pohs lee•toor•<u>ghee</u>…*
the air-conditioner	**το κλιματιστικό** *toh klee•mah•tees•tee•<u>koh</u>*
the dishwasher	**το πλυντήριο πιάτων** *toh plee•<u>ndee</u>•ree•oh <u>piah</u>•tohn*
the freezer	**ο καταψύκτης** *oh kah•tah•<u>psee</u>•ktees*
the heater	**ο θερμοσίφωνας** *oh thehr•moh•<u>see</u>•foh•nahs*
the microwave	**ο φούρνος μικροκυμάτων** *oh <u>foor</u>•nohs meek•roh•kee•<u>mah</u>•tohn*
the refrigerator	**το ψυγείο** *toh psee•<u>ghee</u>•oh*

In Greece the electricity supply is 220 V, with standard continental 2-pin or 3-pin plugs. A multi-adapter is recommended.

Are there...?	**Υπάρχουν...;** *ee-pahr-hoon...*
cooking facilities	**ηλεκτρική κουζίνα** *ee-lehk-tree-kee koo-zee-nah*
electrical outlets	**πρίζες** *pree-zehs*
laundry facilities	**πλυντήρια** *pleen-dee-ree-ah*
showers	**ντους** *dooz*
tents for hire	**σκηνές για ενοικίαση** *skee-nehs yah eh-nee-kee-ah-see*
Where can I empty the chemical toilet?	**Πού μπορώ να αδειάσω τη χημική τουαλέτα;** *poo bohroh nah ah-THee-ah-soh tee khee-mee-kee too ah-leh-tah*

Communications

ESSENTIAL

Where's an internet cafe?	**Πού υπάρχει internet cafe;** *poo ee-pahr-khee een-tehr-neht kah-feh*
Can I access the internet/check e-mail here?	**Μπορώ να μπω στο internet/να ελέγξω τα e-mail μου εδώ;** *boh-roh nah boh stoh een-tehr-neht/nah eh-lehng-ksoh tah ee-meh-eel moo eh-THoh*
How much per hour/half hour?	**Πόσο χρεώνεται η ώρα/μισή ώρα;** *poh-soh hreh-oh-neh-teh ee oh-rah/mee-see oh-rah*
How do I connect/log on?	**Πώς μπορώ να συνδεθώ/μπω;** *pohs boh-roh nah seehn-THeh-thoh/ boh*
I'd like a phone card.	**Θα ήθελα μια τηλεκάρτα.** *thah ee-theh-lah miah tee-leh-kahr-tah*
Can I have your phone number?	**Μπορώ να έχω τον αριθμό τηλεφώνου σας;** *boh-roh nah eh-hoh tohn ah-reeth-moh tee-leh-foh-noo sahs*
Here's my number /e-mail address.	**Ορίστε το τηλέφωνό μου/e-mail μου.** *oh-rees-teh toh tee-leh-foh-noh moo/ee-meh-eel moo*
Call me.	**Πάρτε με τηλέφωνο.** *pahr-teh meh tee-leh-foh-noh*

E-mail me.	**Στείλτε μου e-mail.** _steel_·teh moo ee·_meh_·eel
Hello. This is…	**Εμπρός. Είμαι…** ehm·_brohs_ ee·_meh_…
I'd like to speak to…	**Θα ήθελα να μιλήσω με…** thah ee·theh·lah nah mee·_lee_·soh meh…
Repeat that, please.	**Επαναλάβετέ το, παρακαλώ.** eh·pah·nah·lah·veh·_teh_ toh pah·rah·kah·_loh_
I'll be in touch.	**Θα επικοινωνήσω μαζί σας.** thah eh·pee·kee·noh·_nee_·soh mah·_zee_ sahs
Bye.	**Αντίο.** ah·_dee_·oh
Where is the nearest/ main post office?	**Πού είναι το κοντινότερο/κεντρικό ταχυδρομείο;** poo ee·neh toh koh·ndee·_noh_·teh·roh/kehn·dree·_koh_ tah·khee·THroh·_mee_·oh
I'd like to send this to…	**Θα ήθελα να στείλω αυτό σε…** thah ee·theh·lah nah _stee_·loh ahf·_toh_ seh…

Online

Where's an internet cafe?	**Πού υπάρχει ένα internet cafe;** poo ee·_pahr_·khee eh·nah een·tehr·_neht_ kah·_feh_
Does it have wireless internet?	**Έχει ασύρματο internet;** eh·khee ah·_seer_·mah·toh een·tehr·_neht_
What is the WiFi password?	**Ποιος είναι ο κωδικός πρόσβασης για το WiFi;** piohs ee·neh oh koh·THee·_kohs_ proh·svah·sees yah toh WiFi
Is the WiFi free?	**Το WiFi είναι δωρεάν;** toh WiFi ee·neh THo·reh·_ahn_
Do you have bluetooth?	**Έχετε bluetooth;** eh·kheh·teh bluetooth
How do I turn the computer on/off?	**Πώς ανοίγει/κλείνει ο υπολογιστής;** pohs ah·_nee_·ghee/_klee_·nee oh ee·poh·loh·ghees·_tees_
Can I…?	**Μπορώ…;** boh·_roh_…
access the internet here	**να έχω πρόσβαση στο internet από εδώ** nah eh·hoh _prohs_·vah·see stoh een·tehr·_neht_ ah·_poh_ eh·_THoh_

YOU MAY HEAR...

Ποιος είστε; *piohs ee·steh* — Who's calling?

Περιμένετε, παρακαλώ. *peh·ree·meh·neh·the pah·rah·kah·loh* — Hold on, please.

Θα σας συνδέσω. *thah sahs seen·THeh·soh* — I'll put you through.

Θέλετε να αφήσετε μήνυμα; *theh·leh·teh nah ah·fee·seh·teh mee·nee·mah* — Would you like to leave a message?

Ξανακαλέστε αργότερα/σε δέκα λεπτά. *ksah·nah·kah·lehs·teh ahr·ghoh·teh·rah/she eh·kah lehp·tah* — Call back later/in ten minutes.

Να σας πάρει εκείνος/εκείνη; *nah sahs pah·ree eh·kee·nohs/eh·kee·nee* — Can he/she call you back?

Ποιος είναι ο αριθμός σας; *piohs ee·neh oh ah·reeth·mohs sahs* — What's your number?

Phone

A phone card/ prepaid phone, please.	**Μια τηλεκάρτα/χρονοκάρτα.** *miah tee·leh·kahr·tah/khroh·noh·kahr·tah*	
How much?	**Πόσο;** *poh·soh*	
Where's the pay phone?	**Πού είναι ένα καρτοτηλέφωνο;** *poo ee·neh toh kahr·toh·tee·leh·foh·noh*	
What's the area/ country code for...?	**Ποιος είναι ο κωδικός περιοχής/χώρας για...;** *piohs ee·neh oh koh·THee·kohs peh·ree·oh·khees/khoh·rahs yah...*	
What's the number for Information?	**Ποιος είναι ο αριθμός για Πληροφορίες;** *piohs ee·neh oh ah·reeth·mohs yah plee·roh·foh·ree·ehs*	
I'd like the number for...	**Θα ήθελα έναν αριθμό για...** *thah ee·theh·lah eh·nahn ah·reeth·moh yah...*	

I'd like to call collect [reverse the charges].	**Θέλω να τηλεφωνήσω με αναστροφή χρέωσης.** *theh·loh nah tee·leh·foh·nee·soh meh ah·nah·stroh·fee khreh·oh·sees*
My phone doesn't work here	**Το τηλέφωνό μου δεν λειτουργεί εδώ.** *toh tee·leh·foh·noh moo THehn lee·toor·ghee eh·THoh*
What network are you on?	**Σε ποιο δίκτυο είσαι;** *seh pioh THee·ktee·oh ee·seh*
Is it 3G?	**Είναι 3G;** *ee·neh 3G*
I have run out of credit/minutes.	**Δεν έχω μονάδες/λεπτά.** *THehn eh·khoh moh·nah·THehs/leh·ptah*
Can I buy some credit?	**Μπορώ να αγοράσω μονάδες;** *boh·roh nah ah·ghoh·rah·soh moh·nah·THehs*
Do you have a phone charger?	**Έχετε φορτιστή για τηλέφωνο;** *eh·kheh·teh foh·rtee·stee yah tee·leh·foh·noh*
Can I have your number?	**Μπορώ να έχω τον αριθμό τηλεφώνου σας;** *boh·roh nah eh·khoh tohn ah·reeth·moh tee·leh·foh·noo sahs*
Here's my number.	**Ορίστε ο αριθμός τηλεφώνου μου.** *oh·ree·steh oh ah·reeth·mohs tee·leh·foh·noo moo*
Please text me.	**Παρακαλώ, στείλτε μου μήνυμα.** *pah·rah·kah·loh steel·teh moo mee·nee·mah*
I'll call you.	**Θα σας πάρω τηλέφωνο.** *thah sahs pah·rohtee·leh·foh·noh*

Throughout Greece, even in remote areas, there are plenty of public phones; these are mainly card operated. Phone cards can be purchased from **περίπτερα** *(peh·ree·pteh·rah)*, kiosks. You can also purchase a **κάρτα για κινητό** *(kah·rtah yiah kee·nee·toh)* prepaid card for your wireless phone from any of the conveniently located wireless phone stores.

Food & Drink

ESSENTIAL

Can you recommend a good restaurant/bar?	**Μπορείτε να συστήσετε ένα καλό εστιατόριο/ μπαρ;** boh·_ree_·teh nah sees·_tee_·seh·teh _eh_·nah kah·_loh_ ehs·tee·ah·_toh_·ree·oh/bahr
Is there a traditional Greek/ an inexpensive restaurant near here?	**Υπάρχει κανένα ελληνικό/φθηνό εστιατόριο εδώ κοντά;** ee·_pahr_·khee kah·_neh_·nah eh·lee·nee·_koh_/ fthee·_noh_ ehs·tee·ah·_toh_·ree·oh eh·_THoh_ kohn·_dah_
A table for..., please.	**Ένα τραπέζι για..., παρακαλώ.** _eh_·nah trah·_peh_·zee yah...pah·rah·kah·_loh_
Could we sit...?	**Μπορούμε να καθήσουμε...;** boh·_roo_·meh nah kah·_thee_·soo·meh...
here/there	**εδώ/εκεί** eh·_THoh_/eh·_kee_
outside	**έξω** _eh_·ksoh
in a non-smoking area	**σε έναν χώρο για μη καπνίζοντες** seh _eh_·nahnk hoh· roh yah mee kahp·_nee_·zohn·dehs
I'm waiting for someone.	**Περιμένω κάποιον.** peh·ree·_meh_·noh _kah_·piohn
Where are the toilets	**Πού είναι η τουαλέτα;** poo _ee_·neh ee too·ah·_leh_·tah
A menu, please.	**Έναν κατάλογο, παρακαλώ.** _eh_·nahn kah·_tah_·loh· ghoh pah·rah·kah·_loh_
What do you recommend?	**Τι προτείνετε;** tee proh·_tee_·neh·the
I'd like...	**Θα ήθελα...** thah _ee_·theh·lah...
Some more..., please.	**Λίγο ακόμη..., παρακαλώ.** _lee_·ghoh ah·_koh_·mee... pah·rah·kah·_loh_
Enjoy your meal!	**Καλή όρεξη!** kah·_lee_ oh·reh·ksee

in the shade	**στη σκιά** *stee skee·ah*
in the sun	**στον ήλιο** *stohn ee·lioh*
Where is the restroom [toilet]?	**Πού είναι η τουαλέτα;** *poo ee·neh ee too·ah·leh·tah*

How to Order

Waiter!/Waitress!	**Γκαρσόν!/Δεσποινίς!** *gahr·sohn/THehs·pee·nees*
We're ready to order.	**Είμαστε έτοιμοι να παραγγείλουμε.** *ee·mahs·teh eh·tee·mee nah pah·rah·gee·loo·meh*
May I see the wine list?	**Μπορώ να δω τον κατάλογο κρασιών;** *boh·roh nah THoh tohn kah·tah·loh·ghoh krah·siohn*
I'd like...	**Θα ήθελα...** *thah ee·theh·lah...*
a bottle of...	**ένα μπουκάλι...** *eh·nah boo·kah·lee...*
carafe of...	**μια καράφα...** *miah kah·rah·fah...*
glass of...	**ένα ποτήρι...** *eh·nah poh·tee·ree...*
The menu, please.	**Τον κατάλογο, παρακαλώ.** *tohn kah·tah·loh·ghoh pah·rah·kah·loh*
Do you have...?	**Έχετε...;** *eh·kheh·teh...*
a menu in English	**έναν κατάλογο στα Αγγλικά** *eh·nahn kah·tah·loh·ghoh stah ahng·lee·kah*
a fixed-price menu	**έναν κατάλογο με σταθερές τιμές** *eh·nahnkah·tah·loh·ghoh meh stah·theh·rehs tee·mehs*
a children's menu	**παιδικό μενού** *peh·THee·koh meh·noo*
What do you recommend?	**Τι προτείνετε;** *tee proh·tee·neh·the*
What's this?	**Τι είναι αυτό;** *tee ee·neh ahf·toh*
What's in it?	**Τι περιέχει;** *tee peh·ree·eh·khee*
Is it spicy?	**Είναι πικάντικο;** *ee·neh pee·kahn·dee·koh*
I'd like...	**Θα ήθελα...** *thah ee·theh·lah...*
More..., please.	**Λίγο ακόμη..., παρακαλώ.** *lee·ghoh ah·koh·mee... pah·rah·kah·loh*

With/Without…	**Με/Χωρίς…** *meh/khoh•rees…*
I can't have…	**Δεν πρέπει να φάω φαγητό που περιέχει…** *THehn preh•pee nah fah•oh fah•yee•toh poo peh•ree•eh•khee…*
rare	**με το αίμα του, σενιάν** *meh toh eh•mah too seh•nian*
medium	**μέτρια ψημένο** *meht•ree•ah psee•meh•noh*
well-done	**καλοψημένο** *kah•loh•psee•meh•noh*
It's to go [take away].	**Είναι για το σπίτι.** *ee•neh yah toh spee•tee*

YOU MAY SEE…

ΚΟΥΒΕΡ *koo•vehr*	cover charge
ΣΤΑΘΕΡΗ ΤΙΜΗ *stah•theh•ree tee•mee*	fixed-price
ΚΑΤΑΛΟΓΟΣ *kah•tah•loh•ghohs*	menu
ΜΕΝΟΥ ΤΗΣ ΗΜΕΡΑΣ *meh•noo tees ee•meh•rahs*	menu of the day
Η ΕΞΥΠΗΡΕΤΗΣΗ (ΔΕΝ) ΠΕΡΙΛΑΜΒΑΝΕΤΑΙ *ee eh•ksee•pee•reh•tee•see (THehn) peh•ree•lahm•vahn•eh•the*	service (not) included
ΠΙΑΤΑ ΤΗΣ ΗΜΕΡΑΣ *pee•ah•tah tees ee•meh•rahs*	specials

Cooking Methods

baked	**του φούρνου** *too foor•noo*
barbecued, grilled	**της σχάρας** *tees skhah•rahs*
boiled	**βραστό** *vrah•stoh*
braised	**κατσαρόλας** *kah•tsah•roh•lahs*

| Where can I feed/ change the baby? | **Πού μπορώ να ταΐσω/αλλάξω το μωρό;** *poo boh-roh nah tah-ee-soh/ah-lah-ksoh toh moh-roh* |
| Can you warm this? | **Μπορείτε να το ζεστάνετε;** *boh-ree-teh nah toh zehs-tah-neh-teh* |

For Traveling with Children, see page 133.

How to Complain

How much longer will our food be?	**Πόση ώρα ακόμη θα κάνει το φαγητό;** *poh-see oh-rah ah-koh-mee thah kah-nee toh fah-yee-toh*
We can't wait any longer.	**Δεν μπορούμε να περιμένουμε άλλο.** *THehn boh-roo-meh nah peh-ree-meh-noo-meh ah-loh*
We're leaving.	**Φεύγουμε.** *fehv-ghoo-meh*
That's not what I ordered.	**Δεν παρήγγειλα αυτό.** *THehn pah-ree-ngee-lah ahf-toh*
I asked for...	**Ζήτησα...** *zee-tee-sah...*
I can't eat this.	**Δεν μπορώ να το φάω.** *THehn boh-roh nah toh fah-oh*
This is too...	**Αυτό είναι πολύ...** *ahf-toh ee-neh poh-lee...*
cold/hot	**κρύο/ζεστό** *kree-oh/zehs-toh*
salty/spicy	**αλμυρό/πικάντικο** *ahl-mee-roh/pee-kahn-dee-koh*
tough/bland	**σκληρό/ανάλατο** *sklee-roh/ahl-mee-roh*
This isn't clean/ fresh.	**Αυτό δεν είναι καθαρό/φρέσκο.** *ahf-toh THehn ee-neh kah- thah-roh/frehs-koh*

Paying

The check [bill], please.	**Τον λογαριασμό, παρακαλώ.** *tohn loh-ghahr-yahs-moh pah-rah-kah-loh*
We'd like to pay separately.	**Θα πληρώσουμε ξεχωριστά.** *thah plee-roh-soo-meh kseh-khoh-rees-tah*
It's all together.	**Όλοι μαζί.** *oh-lee mah-zee*
Is service included?	**Συμπεριλαμβάνεται και το σέρβις;** *seem-beh-ree- lahm-vah-neh-teh keh toh sehr-vees*
What's this amount for?	**Τί είναι αυτό το ποσό;** *tee ee-neh ahf-toh toh poh-soh*

In Greek restaurants the service charge is included in the price. However, it is still customary to leave a little extra if you are satisfied with the service.

I didn't have that. I had…	**Δεν πήρα αυτό. Πήρα…** THehn pee·rah ahf·toh pee·rah…
Can I pay by credit card?	**Μπορώ να πληρώσω με αυτήν την πιστωτική κάρτα;** boh·roh nah plee·roh·soh meh ahf·teen teen pees·toh·tee·kee kahr·tah
Can I have an itemized bill/a receipt?	**Μπορώ να έχω έναν αναλυτικό λογαριασμό/ μια αναλυτική απόδειξη;** boh·roh nah eh·khoh eh·nahn ah·nah·lee·tee·koh loh·ghahr·yahs·moh/miah ah·nah·lee·tee·kee ah·poh·ee·ksee
That was a delicious meal.	**Ήταν ένα πολύ νόστιμο γεύμα.** ee·tahn eh·nah poh·lee nohs·tee·moh yehv·mah
I've already paid	**Πλήρωσα ήδη** plee·roh·sah ee·THee ↘

Meals & Cooking

Breakfast

bacon	**μπέικον** beh·ee·kohn
bread	**ψωμί** psoh·mee
butter	**βούτυρο** voo·tee·roh
cereal (cold/hot)	**δημητριακά με (ζεστό/κρύο) γάλα** THee·meet·ree·ah·kah meh (zehs·toh/kree·oh) ghah·lah
cheese	**τυρί** tee·ree
coffee/tea	**καφέ/τσάι** kah·feh/tsah·ee
cold cuts [charcuterie]	**αλλαντικά** ah·lah·ndee·kah

pâté	**πατέ** pah-teh
spinach and feta in pastry dough	**σπανακόπιττα** spah-nah-koh-pee-tah
stuffed grape leaves	**ντολμαδάκι** dohl-mah-THah-kee
yogurt, garlic and cucumber dip	**τζατζίκι** jah-jee-kee

A traditional and very tasty egg dish in Greece is **στραπατσάδα** (strah-pah-tsah-THah), scrambled eggs with fresh tomato, but sometimes with other ingredients depending on the region. Another traditional method of using egg is in **αυγολέμονο** (ahv-ghoh-leh-moh-noh): egg yolk and lemon are added to a sauce or soup. This sauce usually accompanies warm stuffed grape leaves and other vegetable dishes or stews.

Soup

bean soup with tomatoes and parsley	**φασολάδα** fah-soh-lah-THah
chicken soup	**κοτόσουπα** koh-toh-soo-pah
chickpea soup	**ρεβύθια σούπα** reh-vee-thiah soo-pah
cracked wheat soup	**τραχανάς** trah-khah-nahs
fish soup thickened with egg and lemon	**ψαρόσουπα αυγολέμονο** psah-roh-soo-pah ahv-ghoh-leh-moh-noh
fish stew with tomatoes	**κακαβιά** kah-kahv-yah
lentil soup	**φακές σούπα** fah-kehs soo-pah
meat soup	**κρεατόσουπα** kreh-ah-toh-soo-pah
soup with rice, eggs	**σούπα αυγολέμονο** soo-pah ahv-ghoh-leh-moh-noh

and lemon juice		
tripe soup	**πατσάς** *pah-tsahs*	
tahini (sesame paste) soup	**ταχινόσουπα** *tah-khee-noh-soo-pah*	
tomato soup	**τοματόσουπα** *toh-mah-toh-soo-pah*	
vegetable soup	**χορτόσουπα** *khohr-toh-soo-pah*	

Fish & Seafood

anchovy	**αντσούγια** *ahn-joo-yahs*
crab	**καβούρι** *kah-voo-ree*
cuttlefish	**σουπιά** *soo-piah*
eel	**χέλι** *kheh-lee*
fresh cod	**μπακαλιάρος** *bah-kah-liah-rohs*
grouper	**σφυρίδα** *sfee-ree-THah*
mullet	**κέφαλος** *keh-fah-lohs*
lobster	**αστακός** *ahs-tah-kohs*
marinated mullet, sole or mackerel	**ψάρι μαρινάτο** *psah-ree mah-ree-nah-toh*
mussels	**μύδι** *mee-THee*
octopus	**χταπόδι** *khtah-poh-THee*
oyster	**στρείδι** *stree-THee*
red mullet	**μπαρμπούνι** *bahr-boo-nee*
salted cod	**μπακαλιάρος παστός** *bah-kah-liah-rohs pahs-tohs*
sardine	**σαρδέλα** *sahr-THeh-lah*
shrimp [prawn]	**γαρίδα** *ghah-ree-THah*
sole	**γλώσσα** *ghloh-sah*
squid	**καλαμάρι** *kah-lah-mah-ree*
swordfish	**ξιφίας** *ksee-fee-ahs*
tuna	**τόννος** *toh-nohs*

Meat & Poultry

beef	**βοδινό**	voh·THee·_noh_
beef or veal stewed with tomatoes and eggplant [aubergine]	**μελιτζανάτο**	meh·lee·jah·_nah_·toh
brains	**μυαλό**	miah·_loh_
Greek burger	**μπιφτέκι**	beef·_teh_·kee
chicken	**κοτόπουλο**	koh·_toh_·poo·loh
cutlet	**κοτολέτα**	koh·toh·_leh_·tah
duck	**πάπια**	_pah_·piah
fillet	**φιλέτο**	fee·_leh_·toh
goat	**κατσικάκι**	kah·tsee·_kah_·kee
goose	**χήνα**	_khee_·nah
ham	**ζαμπόν**	zahm·_bohn_
kidney	**νεφρό**	neh·_froh_
lamb	**αρνί**	ahr·_nee_
liver	**συκώτι**	see·_koh_·tee
layers of eggplant [aubergine], meat and white sauce	**μουσακάς**	moo·sah·_kahs_
meat with orzo pasta baked with tomatoes	**γιουβέτσι**	yoo·_veh_·tsee
pheasant	**φασιανός**	fah·siah·_nohs_
pork	**χοιρινό**	khee·ree·_noh_
rabbit	**κουνέλι**	koo·_neh_·lee
sausage	**λουκάνικο**	loo·_kah_·nee·koh
skewered pork or lamb, cooked over charcoal	**κοντοσούβλι**	koh·ndoh·_soov_·lee dohs

spiced lamb and potatoes baked in parchment or in filo pastry	**αρνάκι εξοχικό** *ahr·nah·kee eh·ksoh·khee·koh*
turkey	**γαλοπούλα** *ghah·loh·poo·lah*
veal	**μοσχάρι** *mohs·khah·ree*
veal/pork steak	**μπριζόλα μοσχαρίσια/χοιρινή** *bree·zoh·lah mohs·khah·ree·siah/khee·ree·nee*

Vegetables & Staples

artichokes	**αγκινάρες** *ahn·gkee·nah·rehs*
asparagus	**σπαράγγια** *spah·rahn·giah*
bay leaf	**δαφνόφυλλο** *THah·fnoh·fee·loh*
basil	**βασιλικός** *vah·see·lee·kohs*
bread	**ψωμί** *psoh·mee*
broad beans	**κουκί** *koo·kee*
butter bean	**φασόλι γίγαντας** *fah·soh·lee yee·ghahn·dahs*
cabbage	**λάχανο** *lah·khah·noh*
carrot	**καρότο** *kah·roh·toh*
cauliflower	**κουνουπίδι** *koo·noo·pee·THee*
celery	**σέλερι** *seh·leh·ree*
cinnamon	**κανέλλα** *kah·neh·lah*
cucumber	**αγγούρι** *ahn·goo·ree*
dill	**άνηθος** *ah·nee·thohs*
eggplant [aubergine]	**μελιτζάνα** *meh·lee·jah·nah*
garlic	**σκόρδο** *skohr·THoh*
green bean	**φασολάκι** *fah·soh·lah·kee*
green peppers	**πιπεριές πράσινες** *pee·pehr·yehs prah·see·nehs*
leek	**πράσο** *prah·soh*
mastic	**μαστίχα** *mahs·tee·khah*
mint	**δυόσμος** *THee·ohz·mohs*

YOU MAY SEE...

ΑΝΑΛΩΣΗ ΚΑΤΑ ΠΡΟΤΙΜΗΣΗ ΠΡΙΝ ΑΠΟ... *ah·nah·loh·see kah·tah proh·tee· mee·see preen ah·poh*	best before...
ΘΕΡΜΙΔΕΣ *thehr·mee·THehs*	calories
ΧΩΡΙΣ ΛΙΠΑΡΑ *khoh·rees lee·pah·rah*	fat free
ΔΙΑΤΗΡΕΙΤΑΙ ΣΤΟ ΨΥΓΕΙΟ *THee·ah·tee·ree·teh stoh psee·yee·oh*	keep refrigerated
ΜΠΟΡΕΙ ΝΑ ΠΕΡΙΕΧΕΙ ΙΧΝΗ ΑΠΟ... *boh·ree nah peh· ree·eh·khee eekh·nee ah·poh...*	may contain traces of...
για φούρνο μικροκυμάτων *yah foo·rnoh mee·kroh· kee·mah·tohn*	microwaveable
πώληση μέχρι... *poh·lee·see meh·khree*	sell by...
κατάλληλο για χορτοφάγους *kah·tah·lee·loh yah khoh· rtoh·fah·ghoos*	suitable for vegetarians

In the Kitchen

bottle opener	**τιρμπουσόν**	teer·mboo·<u>sohn</u>
bowls	**τα μπωλ**	tah bohl
can opener	**ανοιχτήρι**	ah·neekh·<u>tee</u>·ree
corkscrew	**τιρμπουσόν**	teer·boo·<u>sohn</u>
cups	**τα φλυτζάνια**	tah flee·<u>jah</u>·niah
forks	**τα πηρούνια**	tah pee·<u>roo</u>·niah
frying pan	**τηγάνι**	tee·<u>ghah</u>·nee
glasses	**τα ποτήρια**	tah poh·<u>teer</u>·yah
knives	**τα μαχαίρια**	tah mah·<u>khehr</u>·yah
measuring cup/ spoon	**μεζούρα φλυτζάνι/κουτάλι**	meh·<u>zoo</u>·rah flee·<u>jah</u>·nee/koo·<u>tah</u>·lee
napkin	**χαρτοπετσέτα**	khahr·toh·peh·<u>tseh</u>·tah
plates	**τα πιάτα**	tah <u>piah</u>·tah
pot	**κανάτα**	kah·<u>nah</u>·tah
saucepan	**κατσαρόλα**	kah·tsah·<u>roh</u>·lah
spatula	**σπάτουλα**	<u>spah</u>·too·lah
spoons	**κουτάλια**	koo·<u>tah</u>·liah

beef	**βοδινό**	voh·THee·noh
beef or veal stewed with tomatoes and eggplant [aubergine]	**μελιτζανάτο**	meh·lee·jah·nah·toh
beer	**μπίρα**	bee·rah
brains	**μυαλό**	miah·loh
bread	**ψωμί**	psoh·mee
bread roll	**ψωμάκι**	psoh·mah·kee
broad bean	**κουκί**	koo·kee
butter	**βούτυρο**	voo·tee·roh
butter bean	**φασόλι γίγαντας**	fah·soh·lee yee·ghahn·dahs
cabbage	**λάχανο**	lah·khah·noh
candy [sweets]	**καραμέλα**	kah·rah·meh·lah
caramel custard	**κρέμα καραμελέ**	kreh·mah kah·rah·meh·leh
carrot	**καρότο**	kah·roh·toh
cauliflower	**κουνουπίδι**	koo·noo·pee·THee
celery	**σέλερι**	seh·leh·ree
cereal (cold/hot)	**δημητριακά με (ζεστό/κρύο) γάλα**	THee·meet·ree·ah·kah meh (zehs·toh/kree·oh) ghah·lah
cheese	**τυρί**	tee·ree
cheese omelet	**ομελέττα με τυρί**	oh·meh·leh·tah meh tee·ree
cherry	**κεράσι**	keh·rah·see
chicken	**κοτόπουλο**	koh·toh·poo·loh
chicken soup	**κοτόσουπα**	koh·toh·soo·pah
chickpea soup	**ρεβύθια σούπα**	reh·vee·thiah soo·pah
chilled	**παγωμένο**	pah·ghoh·meh·noh
cinnamon	**κανέλλα**	kah·neh·lah
club soda	**σόδα**	soh·THah
coffee	**καφέ**	kah·fehs
cold cuts [charcuterie]	**αλλαντικά**	ah·lah·ndee·kah
cold meat	**κρύο κρέας**	kree·oh kreh·ahs

cottage cheese	**τυρί κότατζ**	tee·_ree_ koh·_tuhtz_
crab	**καβούρι**	kah·_voo_·ree
cracked wheat soup	**τραχανάς**	trah·khah·_nahs_
cream	**κρέμα**	_kreh_·mah
cucumber	**αγγούρι**	ahn·_goo_·ree
cutlet	**κοτολέτα**	koh·toh·_leh_·tah
cuttlefish	**σουπιά**	soo·_piah_
date	**χουρμάς**	khoor·_mahs_
dill	**άνηθος**	_ah_·nee·thohs
draft	**βαρελίσια**	vah·reh·_lee_·siah
duck	**πάπια**	_pah_·piah
eel	**χέλι**	_kheh_·lee
egg	**αυγό**	ahv·_ghoh_
eggplant [aubergine]	**μελιτζάνα**	meh·lee·_jah_·nah
fig	**σύκο**	_see_·koh
fillet	**φιλέτο**	fee·_leh_·toh
filo pastry filled with almonds, orange juice and cinnamon	**κοπεγχάγη**	koh·pehn·_khah_·ghee
filo pastry filled with custard and steeped in syrup	**γαλακτομπούρεκο**	ghah·lah·ktoh·_boo_·reh·koh
fish	**ψάρι**	_psah_·ree
fish soup thickened with egg and lemon	**ψαρόσουπα αυγολέμονο**	psah·_roh_·soo·pah ahv·ghoh·_leh_·moh·noh
fish stew with tomatoes	**κακαβιά**	kah·kahv·_yah_
fresh cod	**μπακαλιάρος**	bah·kah·_liah_·rohs
fried baby squid	**καλαμαράκια**	kah·lah·mah·_rah_·kiah
fried meatballs	**κεφτεδάκια**	kef·teh·_THah_·kiah
fried whitebait	**μαρίδα τηγανητή**	mah·_ree_·THah tee·ghah·nee·_tee_

spinach	**σπανάκι** *spah·nah·kee*
spinach and feta in pastry dough	**σπανακόπιττα** *spah·nah·koh·pee·tah*
stuffed grape leaves	**ντολμαδάκι** *dohl·mah·THah·kee*
squid	**καλαμάρι** *kah·lah·mah·ree*
steak	**μπριζόλα** *bree·zoh·lah*
sugar	**ζάχαρη** *zah·khah·ree*
swordfish	**ξιφίας** *ksee·fee·ahs*
syrup	**σιρόπι** *see·roh·pee*
tahini (sesame paste) soup	**ταχινόσουπα** *tah·khee·noh·soo·pah*
tangerine	**μανταρίνι** *mahn·dah·ree·nee*
taramosalata, fish roe dip	**ταραμοσαλάτα** *tah·rah·moh·sah·lah·tah*
tea	**τσάι** *tsah·ee*
thyme	**θυμάρι** *thee·mah·ree*
toast	**ψωμί φρυγανιά** *psoh·mee free·ghah·niah*
tomato	**ντομάτα** *ndoh·mah·tah*
tomato soup	**τοματόσουπα** *toh·mah·toh·soo·pah*
tongue (meat)	**γλώσσα** *ghloh·sah*
tonic water	**τόνικ** *toh·neek*

tripe soup	**πατσάς** *pah·tsahs*
tuna	**τόννος** *toh·nohs*
turkey	**γαλοπούλα** *ghah·loh·poo·lah*
Turkish delight	**λουκούμι** *loo·koo·mee*
unleavened bread	**λαγάνα** *lah·ghah·nah*
veal	**μοσχάρι** *mohs·khah·ree*
veal steak	**μπριζόλα μοσχαρίσια** *bree·zoh·lah mohs·khah·ree·siah*
vegetable	**λαχανικό** *lah·khah·nee·koh*
vegetable soup	**χορτόσουπα** *khohr·toh·soo·pah*
walnut cake	**καρυδόπιτα** *kah·ree·THoh·pee·tah*
water	**νερό** *neh·roh*
watermelon	**καρπούζι** *kahr·poo·zee*
wheat	**σιτάρι** *see·tah·ree*
wine	**κρασί** *krah·see*
yogurt (with honey)	**γιαούρτι (με μέλι)** *yah·oor·tee (meh meh·lee)*
yogurt, garlic and cucumber dip	**τζατζίκι** *jah·jee·kee*
zucchini [courgette]	**κολοκυθάκι** *koh·loh·kee·thah·kee*

People

ESSENTIAL

Hello.	**Χαίρετε.** _kheh•reh•teh_
How are you?	**Πώς είστε;** _pohs ee•steh_
Fine, thanks. And you?	**Καλά, ευχαριστώ. Εσείς;** _kah•lah ehf•khah•ree•stoh eh•sees_
Excuse me!	**Συγγνώμη!** _seegh•noh•mee_
Do you speak English?	**Μιλάτε Αγγλικά;** _mee•lah•the uhng•lee•kah_
What's your name?	**Πώς λέγεστε;** _pohs leh•yeh•steh_
My name is...	**Λέγομαι...** _leh•ghoh•meh..._
Nice to meet you.	**Χαίρω πολύ.** _kheh•roh poh•lee_
Where are you from?	**Από πού είστε;** _ah•poo poo ee•steh_
I'm from the U.S./U.K.	**Είμαι από τις Ηνωμένες Πολιτείες/το Ηνωμένο Βασίλειο.** _ee•meh ah•poh tees ee•noh•meh•nehs poh•lee•tee•ehs/toh ee•noh•meh•noh vah•see•lee•oh_
What do you do?	**Τι δουλειά κάνετε;** _tee THoo•liah kah•neh•teh_
I work for...	**Δουλεύω για...** _THoo•leh•voh yah..._
I'm a student.	**Είμαι φοιτητής _m_/φοιτήτρια _f._** _ee•meh fee•tee•tees/fee•tee•tree•ah_
I'm retired.	**Είμαι συνταξιούχος.** _ee•meh seen•dah•ksee•oo•khohs_
Do you like...?	**Σου αρέσει...;** _soo ah•reh•see..._
Goodbye.	**Γεια σας.** _yah sahs_
See you later.	**Τα λέμε αργότερα.** _tah leh•meh ahr•ghoh•teh•rah_

work full-/part-time	**δουλεύω με πλήρη/μερική απασχόληση**	THoo•<u>lehv</u>•oh meh <u>plee</u>•ree/meh•ree•<u>kee</u> ah•pah•<u>skhoh</u>•lee•see
am unemployed	**δεν δουλεύω**	THehn THoo•<u>lehv</u>•oh
work at home	**δουλεύω στο σπίτι**	THoo•<u>lehv</u>•oh stoh <u>spee</u>•tee
Who do you work for…?	**Για ποιον δουλεύετε…;**	yah piohn THoo•<u>leh</u>•veh•teh…
I work for…	**Δουλεύω για…**	THoo•<u>leh</u>•voh yah…
Here's my business card.	**Ορίστε η κάρτα μου.**	oh•<u>ree</u>•steh ee <u>kahr</u>•tah moo

Weather

What's the weather forecast for tomorrow?	**Τι λέει η πρόβλεψη του καιρού για αύριο;**	tee <u>leh</u>•ee ee <u>proh</u>•vleh•psee too keh•<u>roo</u> yah <u>ah</u>•vree•oh
What beautiful/ terrible weather!	**Τι ωραίος/απαίσιος καιρός!**	tee oh•<u>reh</u>•ohs/ ah•<u>peh</u>•see•ohs keh•<u>rohs</u>
It's cool/warm.	**Έχει δροσιά/ζέστη.**	<u>eh</u>•khee roh•<u>siah</u>/<u>zeh</u>•stee
It's cold/hot.	**Κάνει κρύο/ζέστη.**	<u>kah</u>•nee <u>kree</u>•oh/<u>zeh</u>•stee
It's rainy/sunny.	**Ο καιρός είναι βροχερός/ηλιόλουστος.**	oh keh•<u>rohs</u> ee•neh vroh•kheh•<u>rohs</u>/ee•<u>lioh</u>•loo•stohs
It's snowy/icy.	**Έχει παγωνιά.**	<u>eh</u>•khee pah•ghoh•<u>niah</u>
Do I need a jacket/ an umbrella?	**Να πάρω ζακέτα/ομπρέλα;**	nah <u>pah</u>•roh zah•<u>keh</u>•tah/ ohm•<u>breh</u>•lah

Romance

ESSENTIAL

Would you like to go out for a drink/ dinner?	**Θέλετε να βγούμε για ποτό/φαγητό;** *theh·leh·teh nah vghoo·meh yah poh·toh/ fah·yee·toh*
What are your plans for tonight/ tomorrow?	**Ποια είναι τα σχέδιά σας για απόψε/αύριο;** *piah ee·neh tah skheh·THee·ah sahs yah ah·poh·pseh/ahv·ree·oh*
Can I have your number?	**Μπορώ να έχω τον αριθμό τηλεφώνου σας;** *boh·roh nah eh·khoh tohn ah·reeth·moh tee· leh·foh·noo sahs*
May we join you?	**Να έρθουμε μαζί σας;** *nah ehr·thoo·meh mah·zee sahs*
Let me buy you a drink.	**Να σε κεράσω ένα ποτό.** *nah seh keh·rah·soh eh·nah poh·toh*
I like you.	**Μου αρέσεις.** *moo ah·reh·sees*
I love you.	**Σ' αγαπώ.** *sah·ghah·poh*

The Dating Game

Would you like to go out for coffee?	**Θα θέλατε να βγούμε για καφέ;** *thah theh·lah·teh nah vghoo·meh yah kah·feh*
Would you like to go out for a drink/to dinner?	**Θέλεις να βγεις για ποτό/φαγητό;** *theh·lees nah vghees yah poh·toh/fah·ghee·toh*
What are your plans for…?	**Ποια είναι τα σχέδιά σας για…;** *piah ee·neh tah skheh·THee·ah sahs yah…*
tonight	**απόψε** *ah·poh·pseh*
tomorrow	**αύριο** *ahv·ree·oh*

this weekend	**αυτό το Σαββατοκύριακο** ahf-<u>toh</u> toh sah-vah-toh-<u>kee</u>-riah-koh
Where would you like to go?	**Πού θα θέλατε να πάμε;** poo thah <u>theh</u>-lah-the nah <u>pah</u>-meh
I'd like to go to...	**Θα ήθελα να πάω...** thah <u>ee</u>-theh-lah nah <u>pah</u>-oh...
Do you like...?	**Σου αρέσει...;** soo ah-<u>reh</u>-see...
Can I have your number/e-mail?	**Μου δίνετε το τηλέφωνο/e-mail σας;** moo <u>THee</u>-neh-teh toh tee-<u>leh</u>-foh-noh/ee-<u>meh</u>-eel sahs
Are you on Facebook/Twitter?	**Είσαι στο Facebook/Twitter;** <u>ee</u>-seh stoh Facebook/Twitter
Can I join you?	**Να έρθω κι εγώ στην παρέα σας;** nah <u>ehr</u>-thoh kee eh-<u>ghoh</u> steen pah-<u>reh</u>-ah sahs
You look great!	**Είστε πολύ όμορφος m /όμορφη f !** <u>ee</u>-steh poh-<u>lee</u> <u>oh</u>-mohr-fohs/<u>oh</u>-mohr-fee
Shall we go somewhere quieter?	**Πάμε κάπου πιο ήσυχα;** <u>pah</u>-meh <u>kah</u>-poo pioh <u>ee</u>-see-khah

For Communications, see page 48.

Accepting & Rejecting

Thank you. I'd love to.	**Ευχαριστώ. Θα το ήθελα πολύ.** ehf-khah-rees-<u>toh</u> thah toh <u>ee</u>-theh-lah poh-<u>lee</u>
Where should we meet?	**Πού θα συναντηθούμε;** poo thah see-nahn-dee-<u>t</u> <u>hoo</u>-meh
I'll meet you at the bar/your hotel.	**Θα σε συναντήσω στο μπαρ/στο ξενοδοχείο σου.** thah seh see-nahn-<u>dee</u>-soh stoh bahr/stoh kseh-noh-THoh-<u>khee</u>-oh soo
I'll come by at...	**Θα περάσω στις...** thah peh-<u>rah</u>-soh stees...
Thank you, but I'm busy.	**Σας ευχαριστώ, αλλά είμαι πολύ απασχολημένος m /απασχολημένη f .** sahs ehf-khah-rees-<u>toh</u> ah-<u>lah</u> ee-meh poh-<u>lee</u> ah-pahs-khoh-lee-<u>meh</u>-nohs/ah-pahs-khoh-lee-<u>meh</u>-nee

I'm not interested.	**Δεν ενδιαφέρομαι.** THehn ehn•THee•ah•_feh_•roh•meh
Leave me alone,	**Σας παρακαλώ, αφήστε με ήσυχο _m_ /**
please!	**ήσυχη _f_ !** sahs pah•rah•kah•_loh_ ah•_fees_•the
	meh _ee_•see•khoh/_ee_•see•khee
Stop bothering me!	**Σταματείστε να με ενοχλείτε!** stah•mah•_tee_•steh nah
	meh eh•noh•_khlee_•the

Getting Intimate

Can I hug/kiss you?	**Μπορώ να σε αγκαλιάσω/φιλήσω;** boh•_roh_ nah seh	99
	ahn•gah•_liah_•soh/fee•_lee_•soh
Yes.	**Ναι.** neh
No.	**Όχι.** _oh_•khee
Stop!	**Σταμάτα!** stah•_mah_•tah
I love you.	**Σ' αγαπώ.** sah•ghah•_poh_

Sexual Preferences

Are you gay?	**Είσαι γκέι;** _ee_•seh _geh_•ee
I'm...	**Είμαι...** _ee_•meh...
heterosexual	**ετεροφυλόφιλος _m_ /ετεροφυλόφιλη _f_** eh•teh•roh•
	fee•_loh_•fee•lohs/eh•teh•roh•fee•_loh_•fee•lee
homosexual	**ομοφυλόφιλος _m_ /ομοφυλόφιλη _f_** oh•moh•fee•_loh_•
	fee•lohs/oh•moh•fee•_loh_•fee•lee
bisexual	**αμφιφυλόφιλος _m_ /αμφιφυλόφιλη _f_** ahm•fee•fee•
	loh•fee•lohs/ahm•fee•fee•_loh_•fee•lee
Do you like	**Σου αρέσουν οι άνδρες/γυναίκες;** soo ah•_reh_•soon
men/women?	ee _ahn_•THrehs/ghee•_neh_•kehs

For Grammar, see page 151.

The official, government-run tourist information offices are known as **ΕΟΤ** *(eh·oht)*, **Ελληνικός Οργανισμός Τουρισμού** *(eh·lee·nee·kohs ohr·ghah·nees·mohs too·rees·moo)*, in Greece and **ΚΟΤ** *(koht)*, **Κυπριακός Οργανισμός Τουρισμού** *(keep·ree·ah·kohs ohr·ghah·nees·mohs too·rees·moo)* in Cyprus. They can be found in most tourist resorts and major towns.

When's the next tour?	**Πότε είναι η επόμενη περιήγηση;** *poh·teh ee·neh ee eh·poh·meh·nee peh·ree·ee·ghee·see*
Are there tours in English?	**Γίνονται ξεναγήσεις στα αγγλικά;** *ghee·nohn·deh kseh·nah·yee·sees stah ahng·lee·kah*
What time do we leave/return?	**Τι ώρα αναχωρούμε/επιστρέφουμε;** *tee oh·rah ah·nah·khoh·roo·meh/eh·pees·treh·foo·meh*
We'd like to have a look at the...	**Θα θέλαμε να ρίξουμε μια ματιά...** *thah theh·lah·meh nah ree·ksoo·meh miah mah·tiah...*
Can we stop here...?	**Μπορούμε να σταματήσουμε εδώ...;** *boh·roo·meh nah stah·mah·tee·soo·meh eh·THoh...*
to take photographs	**για να βγάλουμε φωτογραφίες** *yah nah vghah·loo·meh foh·toh·ghrah·fee·ehs*
to buy souvenirs	**για να αγοράσουμε σουβενίρ** *yah nah ah·ghoh·rah·soo·meh soo·veh·neer*
to use the restroom [toilet]	**για τουαλέτα** *yah too·ah·leh·tah*
Is there access for the disabled?	**Υπάρχει πρόσβαση για άτομα με ειδικές ανάγκες;** *ee·pahr·khee prohz·vah·see yah ah·toh·mah meh ee·THee·kehs ah·nahn·gehs*

For Tickets, see page 19.

Seeing the Sights

Where is…?	**Πού είναι…;**	poo ee·neh…
the battleground	**το πεδίο μάχης**	toh peh·THee·oh mah·khees
the botanical garden	**ο βοτανικός κήπος**	oh voh·tah·nee·kohs kee·pohs
the castle	**το κάστρο**	toh kahs·troh
Where is…?	**Πού είναι…;**	poo ee·neh…
the downtown area	**το κέντρο της πόλης**	toh kehn·droh tees poh·lees
the fountain	**το συντριβάνι**	toh seen·dree·vah·nee
the library	**η βιβλιοθήκη**	ee veev·lee·oh·thee·kee
the market	**η αγορά**	ee ah·ghoh·rah
the museum	**το μουσείο**	toh moo·see·oh
the old town	**η παλιά πόλη**	ee pah·liah poh·lee
the opera house	**το μέγαρο μουσικής**	toh meh·ghah·roh moo·see·kees
the palace	**τα ανάκτορα**	tah ah·nahk·toh·rah
the park	**το πάρκο**	toh pahr·koh
the ruins	**τα αρχαία**	tah ahr·kheh·ah
the shopping area	**η εμπορική περιοχή**	ee ehm·boh·ree·kee peh·ree·oh·khee
the town hall	**το Δημαρχείο**	toh THee·mahr·khee·oh

Can you show me on the map?	**Μπορείτε να μου δείξετε στο χάρτη;**
	boh•ree•teh nah moo THee•kseh•teh stoh khahr•tee
It's…	**Είναι…** *ee•neh…*
amazing	**καταπληκτικό** *kah•tah•plee•ktee•koh*
beautiful	**όμορφο** *oh•mohr•foh*
boring	**βαρετός** *vah•reh•toh*
interesting	**ενδιαφέρον** *ehn•THee•ah•feh•rohn*
magnificent	**μεγαλοπρεπές** *meh•ghah•lohp•reh•pehs*
romantic	**ρομαντικό** *roh•mahn•dee•koh*
strange	**παράξενο** *pah•rah•kseh•noh*
terrible	**απαίσιο** *ah•peh•see•oh*
ugly	**άσχημο** *ahs•khee•moh*
I (don't) like it.	**(Δεν) Μου αρέσει.** *(THen) moo ah•reh•see*

For Asking Directions, see page 34.

Religious Sites

Where is…?	**Πού είναι…;** *poo ee•neh…*
the cathedral	**ο καθεδρικός** *oh kah•theh•THree•kohs*
the Catholic/ Protestant church	**η καθολική/ προτεσταντική εκκλησία** *ee kah•thoh• lee•kee/proh•teh•stahn•dee•kee ehk•lee•see•ah*
the mosque	**το τζαμί** *toh jah•mee*
the shrine	**ο ιερός χώρος** *oh ee•eh•rohs khoh•rohs*
the synagogue	**η συναγωγή** *ee see•nah•ghoh•yee*
the temple	**ο ναός** *oh nah•ohs*
What time is mass/ the service?	**Τι ώρα είναι η λειτουργία;** *tee oh•rah ee•neh ee lee•toor•yee•ah*

ESSENTIAL

Where is the market/mall?	**Πού είναι η αγορά/το εμπορικό κέντρο;** *poo ee•neh ee ah•ghoh•rah/toh ehm•boh•ree•koh kehn•droh*
I'm just looking.	**Απλώς κοιτάω.** *ahp•lohs kee•tah•oh*
Can you help me?	**Μπορείτε να με βοηθήσετε;** *boh•ree•teh nah meh voh•ee•thee•seh•teh*
I'm being helped.	**Με εξυπηρετούν.** *meh eh•ksee•pee•reh•toon*
How much?	**Πόσο;** *poh•soh*
This/That one, thanks.	**Αυτό/Εκείνο, παρακαλώ.** *ahf•toh/eh•kee•noh pah•rah•kah•loh*
That's all, thanks.	**Τίποτε άλλο, ευχαριστώ.** *tee•poh•teh ah•loh ehf•khah•rees•toh*
Where do I pay?	**Πού πληρώνω;** *poo plee•roh•noh*
I'll pay in cash/by credit card.	**Θα πληρώσω τοις μετρητοίς/με πιστωτική κάρτα.** *thah plee•roh•soh tees meht•ree•tees/meh pees•toh• tee•kee kahr•tah*
A receipt, please.	**Μια απόδειξη, παρακαλώ.** *miah ah•poh•THee•ksee pah•rah•kah•loh*

Shopping can be a great pleasure in Greece. Apart from the standard department stores, you can wander through flea markets and seek out the small handicraft stores that line the narrow alleys of most islands and old towns.

YOU MAY HEAR...

Μπορώ να σας βοηθήσω; *boh·roh*
nah sahs voh·ee·thee·soh

Can I help you?

Μισό λεπτό. *mee·soh lehp·toh*

Just a moment.

Τί θα θέλατε; *tee thah theh·lah·teh*

What would you like?

Τίποτε άλλο; *tee·poh·teh ah·loh*

Anything else?

YOU MAY SEE...

ανοιχτό/κλειστό *ah·nee·khtoh/klee·stoh*	open/closed
κλειστό για το μεσημέρι *klee·stoh yah toh meh·see·meh·ree*	closed for lunch
δοκιμαστήριο *THoh·kee·mah·stee·ree·oh*	fitting room
ταμείο *tah·mee·oh*	cashier
μόνο μετρητά *moh·noh meh·tree·tah*	cash only
δεκτές πιστωτικές κάρτες *THeh·ktehs pee·stoh·tee·kehs kahr·tehs*	credit cards accepted
εργάσιμες ώρες *ehr·ghah·see·mehs oh·rehs*	business hours
έξοδος *eh·ksoh·THohs*	exit

Personal Preferences

I want something...	**Θέλω κάτι...** *theh·loh kah·tee...*
cheap	**φτηνό** *ftee·noh*
expensive	**ακριβό** *ah·ree·voh*
larger	**μεγαλύτερο** *meh·ghah·lee·teh·roh*

smaller	**μικρότερο** meek·roh·teh·roh
from this region	**από αυτό το μέρος** ah·poh uh·toh toh meh·rohs
Around…euros.	**Γύρω στα… ευρώ.** yee·roh stah… ehv·roh
Is it real?	**Είναι αληθινό;** ee·neh ah·lee·thee·noh
Could you show me this/that?	**Μπορείτε να μου δείξετε αυτό/εκείνο;** boh·ree·teh nah moo THee·kseh·teh ahf·toh/eh·kee·noh
That's not quite what I want.	**Δεν είναι ακριβώς αυτό που θέλω.** THehn ee·neh ahk·ree·vohs ahf·toh poo theh·loh
I don't like it.	**Δεν μου αρέσει.** THehn moo ah·reh·see
That's too expensive.	**Είναι πολύ ακριβό.** ee·neh poh·lee ahk·ree·voh
I'd like to think about it.	**Θα ήθελα να το σκεφτώ.** thah ee·theh·lah nah toh skehf·toh
I'll take it.	**Θα το πάρω.** thah toh pah·roh

Paying & Bargaining

How much?	**Πόσο;** poh·soh
I'll pay…	**Θα πληρώσω…** thah plee·roh·soh…
by cash	**τοις μετρητοίς** tees meht·ree·tees
by credit card	**με πιστωτική κάρτα** meh pees·toh·tee·kee kahr·tah
by traveler's check	**με ταξιδιωτική επιταγή** meh tah·ksee·THyo·tee·kee eh·pee·tah·yee
A receipt, please.	**Μια απόδειξη, παρακαλώ.** miah ah·poh·THee·ksee pah·rah·kah·loh
That's too much.	**Είναι πολλά.** ee·neh poh·lah
I'll give you…	**Θα σας δώσω…** thah sahs THoh·soh…
I only have…euros.	**Έχω μόνο…ευρώ.** eh·khoh moh·noh…ehv·roh
Is that your best price?	**Αυτή είναι η καλύτερη τιμή σας;** ahf·tee ee·neh ee kah·lee·teh·ree tee·mee sahs
Can you give me a discount?	**Μπορείτε να μου κάνετε έκπτωση;** boh·ree·teh nah moo kah·neh·teh ehkp·toh·see

For Numbers, see page 156.

YOU MAY HEAR...

Πώς θα πληρώσετε; *pohs thah plee·roh·seh·teh*	How are you paying?
Η πιστωτική σας κάρτα απορρίφθηκε. *ee pee·stoh·tee·kee sahs kahr·tah ah·poh·ree·fthee·keh*	Your credit card has been declined.
Ταυτότητα, παρακαλώ. *tahf·toh·tee·tah, pah·rah·kah·loh*	ID, please.
Δεν δεχόμαστε πιστωτικές κάρτες. *THehn THe·khoh·mah·steh pee·stoh·tee·kehs kahr·tehs*	We don't accept credit cards.
Μόνο μετρητά, παρακαλώ. *moh·noh meht·ree·tah pah·rah·kah·loh*	Cash only, please.
Έχετε ψιλά; *eh·kheh·teh psee·lah*	Do you have any smaller change?

Making a Complaint

I'd like...	**Θα ήθελα...** *thah ee·theh·lah...*
to exchange this	**να αλλάξω αυτό** *nah ah·lah·ksoh ahf·toh*
to return this	**να επιστρέψω αυτό** *nah eh·pees·treh·psoh ahf·toh*
a refund	**επιστροφή των χρημάτων μου** *eh·pees·troh·fee tohn khree·mah·tohn moo*
to see the manager	**να δω τον διευθυντή** *nah THoh tohn THee·ehf·theen·dee*

Services

Can you recommend...?	**Μπορείτε να συστήσετε...;** *boh·ree·teh nah sees·tee·seh·teh...*
a barber	**έναν κουρέα** *eh·nahn koo·reh·ah*
a dry cleaner	**ένα καθαριστήριο** *eh·nah kah·thah·rees·tee·ree·oh*

a hairdresser	**ένα κομμωτήριο** _eh·nah koh·moh·<u>tee</u>·ree·oh_
a laundromat [launderette]	**πλυντήριο ρούχων** _plee·<u>dee</u>·ree·oh_ roo·khohn_
a nail salon	**ένα σαλόνι νυχιών** _eh·nah sah·<u>loh</u>·nee nee·<u>khiohn</u>_
a spa	**ένα σπα** _eh·nah spah_
a travel agency	**ένα ταξιδιωτικό γραφείο** _n eh·nah tah·ksee·THee·oh·tee·<u>koh</u> ghrah·<u>fee</u>·oh_
Can you...this?	**Μπορείτε να...αυτό;** _boh·<u>ree</u>·teh nah...ahf·<u>toh</u>_
alter	**μεταποιήσετε** _meh·tah·pee·<u>ee</u>·seh·teh_
clean	**καθαρίσετε** _kah·thah·<u>ree</u>·seh·teh_
mend	**επιδιορθώσετε** _eh·pee·THee·ohr·<u>thoh</u>·seh·teh_
press	**σιδερώσετε** _see·THeh·<u>roh</u>·seh·teh_
When will it/they be ready?	**Πότε θα είναι έτοιμο/έτοιμα;** _poh·teh thah ee·neh <u>eh</u>·tee·moh/<u>eh</u>·tee·mah_

Hair & Beauty

I'd like...	**Θα ήθελα...** _thah <u>ee</u>·theh·lah..._
an appointment for today/ tomorrow	**να κλείσω ένα ραντεβού για σήμερα/αύριο** _nah <u>klee</u>·soh eh·nah rahn·deh·<u>voo</u> yah <u>see</u>·meh·rah/<u>ahv</u>·ree·oh_
some colour/ highlights	**βαφή/ανταύγειες** _vah·<u>fee</u>/ah·<u>dahv</u>·yehs_
my hair styled/ blow-dried	**ένα χτένισμα/στέγνωμα με πιστολάκι** _eh·nah <u>khteh</u>·nee·smah/steh·ghnoh·mah meh pee·stoh·luh·kee_
a haircut	**ένα κούρεμα** _eh·nah <u>koo</u>·reh·mah_
I'd like...	**Θα ήθελα...** _thah <u>ee</u>·theh·lah..._
an eyebrow/ bikini wax	**χαλάουα στα φρύδια/στο μπικίνι** _khah·<u>lah</u>·oo·ah stah <u>free</u>·yah/stoh bee·<u>kee</u>·nee_
a facial	**έναν καθαρισμό προσώπου** _eh·nahn kah·thah·reez·<u>moh</u> proh·<u>soh</u>·poo_

You will find spas and wellness centers, particularly at luxury hotels, in every major city and on most islands in Greece. You can visit these spas for a full day or for one treatment, without being a guest at the hotel. You will usually have to make an appointment in advance. Tipping is customary, particularly in hair salons, where customers may choose to tip the assistants or trainees.

a manicure/pedicure	**ένα μανικιούρ/πεντικιούρ** *eh·nahmah·nee·kee·oor/pehn·dee·kee·oor*
a (sports) massage	**ένα (αθλητικό) μασάζ** *eh·nah (ahth·lee·tee·koh) mah·sahz*
A trim, please.	**Κόψιμο, παρακαλώ** *koh·psee·moh, pah·rah·kah·loh*
Don't cut it too short.	**Μην τα κόψετε πολύ κοντά.** *meen tah koh·pseh·teh poh·lee kohn·dah*
Shorter here.	**Πιο κοντά εδώ.** *pioh kohn·dah eh·THoh*
Do you do…?	**Κάνετε…;** *kah·neh·teh…*
acupuncture	**βελονισμό** *veh·loh·neez·moh*
aromatherapy	**αρωματοθεραπεία** *ah·roh·mah·toh·theh·rah·pee·ah*
oxygen treatment	**οξυγονοθεραπεία** *oh·ksee·ghoh·noh·theh·rah·pee·ah*
Is there a sauna?	**Υπάρχει σάουνα;** *ee·pahr·kee sah·oo·nah*

Antiques

How old is this?	**Πόσο παλιό είναι αυτό;** *poh·soh pah·lioh ee·neh ahf·toh*
Do you have anything from the…period?	**Έχετε τίποτα από την…περίοδο;** *eh·kheh·teh tee·poh·tah ah·poh teen….peh·ree·oh·THoh*
Do I have to fill out any forms?	**Πρέπει να συμπληρώσω έντυπα;** *preh·pee nah see·blee·roh·soh eh·ndee·pah*

Will I have problems with customs?	**Θα έχω προβλήματα με το τελωνείο;** *thah eh·khoh prohv·lee·mah·tah meh toh teh·loh·nee·oh*
Is there a certificate of authenticity?	**Υπάρχει πιστοποιητικό γνησιότητας;** *ee·pahr·khee pees·toh·pee·ee·tee·koh ghnee·see·oh·tee·tahs*
Can you ship/wrap it?	**Μπορείτε να το στείλετε/τυλίξετε;** *boh·ree·teh nah toh stee·leh·teh/tee·lee·kseh·teh*

Clothing

I'd like...	**Θα ήθελα...** *thah ee·theh·lah...*
Can I try this on?	**Μπορώ να το δοκιμάσω;** *boh·roh nah toh THoh·kee·mah·soh*
It doesn't fit.	**Δεν μου κάνει.** *THehn moo kah·nee*
It's too...	**Είναι πολύ...** *ee·neh poh·lee...*
big	**μεγάλο** *meh·ghah·loh*
small	**μικρό** *meek·roh*
short	**κοντό** *kon·doh*
long	**μακρύ** *mak·ree*
tight	**στενό** *steh·noh*
loose	**φαρδύ** *fahr·THee*
Do you have this in size...?	**Το έχετε στο μέγεθος...;** *toh eh·kheh·teh stoh meh·yeh·thohs...*
Do you have this in a bigger/smaller size?	**Το έχετε σε μεγαλύτερο/μικρότερο μέγεθος;** *kheh·teh seh meh·ghah·lee·teh·roh/meek·roh·teh·roh meh·gheh·thohs*

YOU MAY SEE...

ΑΝΔΡΙΚΑ *ahn·THree·kah*	men's clothing
ΓΥΝΑΙΚΕΙΑ *yee·neh·kee·ah*	women's clothing
ΠΑΙΔΙΚΑ *peh·THee·kah*	children's clothing

Sport & Leisure

ESSENTIAL

When's the game?	**Πότε είναι ο αγώνας;** _poh·teh <u>ee</u>·neh oh ah·<u>ghoh</u>·nahs_
Where's...?	**Πού είναι...;** _poo <u>ee</u>·neh..._
the beach	**η παραλία** _ee pah·rah·<u>lee</u>·ah_
the park	**το πάρκο** _toh <u>pahr</u>·koh_
the pool	**η πισίνα** _ee pee·<u>see</u>·nah_
Is it safe to swim/ dive here?	**Είναι ασφαλές εδώ για κολύμπι/κατάδυση;** _<u>ee</u>·neh ahs·fah·<u>lehs</u> eh·<u>THoh</u> yah koh·<u>leem</u>·bee/ kah·<u>tah</u>·THee·see_
Can I hire golf clubs?	**Μπορώ να νοικιάσω μπαστούνια του γκόλφ;** _boh·<u>roh</u> nah nee·<u>kiah</u>·soh bahs·<u>too</u>·niah too gohlf_
How much per hour?	**Πόσο χρεώνεται η ώρα;** _<u>poh</u>·soh khreh·<u>oh</u>·neh·teh ee <u>oh</u>·rah_
How far is it to...?	**Πόσο μακριά είναι για...;** _<u>poh</u>·soh mahk·ree·<u>ah</u> ee·neh yah..._
Can you show me on the map?	**Μπορείτε να μου δείξετε στο χάρτη;** _boh·<u>ree</u>·teh nah moo <u>THee</u>·kseh·teh stoh <u>khahr</u>·tee_

Watching Sport

When's...	**Πότε είναι...** _poh·teh ee·neh..._
the baseball game	**ο αγώνας μπέιζμπολ** _oh ah·ghoh·nahs beh·ee·zbohl_
the basketball game	**ο αγώνας μπάσκετ** _oh ah·ghoh·nahs bahs·keht_
the boxing match	**ο αγώνας μποξ** _oh ah·ghoh·nahs bohks_
the cricket game	**ο αγώνας κρίκετ** _oh ah·ghoh·nahs kree·keht_
the cycling race	**ο αγώνας ποδηλασίας** _oh ah·ghoh·nahs poh·THee·lah·see·ahs_
the golf tournament	**το τουρνουά γκολφ** _toh toor·noo·ah gohlf_
the soccer [football] game	**ο αγώνας ποδοσφαίρου** _oh ah·ghoh·nahs poh·THohs·feh·roo_
the tennis match	**ο αγώνας τέννις** _oh ah·ghoh·nahs teh·nees_
the volleyball game	**ο αγώνας βόλεϊ** _oh ah·ghoh·nahs voh·leh·ee_
Which teams are playing?	**Ποιες ομάδες παίζουν;** _pee·ehs oh·mah·THehs peh·zoon_
Where's...?	**Πού είναι...;** _poo ee·neh..._
the horse track	**το ιπποδρόμιο** _toh ee·poh·THroh·mee·oh_
the racetrack	**ο ιππόδρομος** _oh ee·poh·THroh·mohs_
the stadium	**το στάδιο** _toh stah·THee·oh_
Where can I place a bet?	**Πού μπορώ να βάλω στοίχημα;** _poo boh·roh nah vah·loh stee·khee·mah_

Playing Sport

Where's...?	**Πού είναι...;** _poo ee·neh..._
the golf course	**το γήπεδο του γκόλφ** _toh yee·peh·THoh too gohlf_
the gym	**το γυμναστήριο** _toh gheem·nahs·tee·ree·oh_
the park	**το πάρκο** _toh pahr·koh_
Where are the tennis courts?	**Πού είναι τα γήπεδα του τέννις;** _poo ee·neh tah ghee·peh·THah too teh·nees_

the forest	**το δάσος** *toh THah•sohs*
the gorge	**το φαράγγι** *toh fah•rah•gee*
the hill	**ο λόφος** *oh loh•fohs*
the lake	**η λίμνη** *ee leem•nee*
the mountain	**το βουνό** *toh voo•noh*
the nature reserve	**ο εθνικός δρυμός** *oh ehth•nee•kohs THree•mohs*
the viewpoint	**η πανοραμική θέση** *ee pah•noh•rah•mee•kee theh•see*
the park	**το πάρκο** *toh pahr•koh*
the path	**το μονοπάτι** *toh moh•noh•pah•tee*
the peak	**η κορυφή** *ee koh•ree•fee*
the picnic area	**η περιοχή για πικ-νικ** *ee peh•ree•oh•khee yah peek•neek*
the pond	**η λίμνη** *ee lee•mnee*
the river	**ο ποταμός** *oh poh•tah•mohs*
the sea	**η θάλασσα** *ee thah•lah•sah*
the thermal bath	**τα ιαματικά λουτρα** *tah ee•ah•mah•tee•kah loot•rah*
the hot spring	**τα ιαματικά λουτρα** *tah ee•ah•mah•tee•kah loot•rah*
the stream	**το ρέμα** *toh reh•mah*
the valley	**η κοιλάδα** *ee kee•lah•THah*
the vineyard	**ο αμπελώνας** *oh ah•beh•loh•nahs*
the volcano	**το ηφαίστειο** *toh ee•feh•stee•oh*
the waterfall	**ο καταρράκτης** *oh kah•tah•rahk•tees*

Going Out

ESSENTIAL

What's there to do in the evenings?	**Τι μπορώ να κάνω τα βράδια;** *tee boh·roh nah kah·noh tah vrahTH·yah*
Do you have a program of events?	**Έχετε ένα πρόγραμμα εκδηλώσεων;** *eh·kheh·teh eh·nah prohgh·rah·mah ehk·THee·loh·seh·ohn*
What's playing at the movies [cinema] tonight?	**Τι παίζει ο κινηματογράφος απόψε;** *tee pch·zee oh kee·nee·mah·tohgh·rah·fohs ah·poh·pseh*
Where's...?	**Πού είναι...;** *poo ee·neh...*
the downtown area	**το κέντρο της πόλης** *toh kehn·droh tees poh·lees*
the bar	**το μπαρ** *toh bahr*
the dance club	**η ντισκοτέκ** *ee dees·koh·tehk*
Is there a cover charge?	**Υπάρχει κουβέρ;** *ee·pahr·hee koo·vehr*

Entertainment

Can you recommend...?	**Μπορείτε να συστήσετε...;** *boh·ree·teh nah sees·tee·seh·teh...*
a concert	**μια συναυλία** *miah see·nahv·lee·ah*
a movie	**μια ταινία** *miah teh·nee·ah*
an opera	**μια όπερα** *miah oh·peh·rah*
a play	**μια θεατρική παράσταση** *miah theh·aht·ree·kee pah·rahs·tah·see* ✓
When does it start/end?	**Πότε αρχίζει/τελειώνει;** *poh·the ahr·khee·zee/ teh·lioh·nee*
What's the dress code?	**Πώς πρέπει να ντυθώ;** *pohs preh·pee nah dee·thoh*
I like...	**Μου αρέσει...** *moo ah·reh·see...*
classical music	**η κλασική μουσική** *ee klah·see·kee moo·see·kee*

Police

ESSENTIAL

Call the police!	**Φωνάξτε την αστυνομία!** *foh·nahks·teh teen ahs·tee·noh·mee·ah*
Where's the nearest police station?	**Πού είναι το κοντινότερο αστυνομικό τμήμα;** *poo ee·neh toh kohn·dee·noh·teh·roh ahs·tee·noh·mee·koh tmee·mah*
There has been an accident.	**Έγινε ένα ατύχημα.** *eh·yee·neh eh·nah ah·tee·khee·mah*
My child is missing.	**Λείπει το παιδί μου.** *lee·pee toh peh·THee moo*
I need...	**Χρειάζομαι...** *khree·ah·zoh·meh...*
an interpreter	**έναν διερμηνέα** *eh·nahn THee·ehr·mee·neh·ah*
I need...	**Χρειάζομαι...** *khree·ah·zoh·meh...*
to contact my lawyer	**να επικοινωνήσω με τον δικηγόρο μου** *nah eh·pee·kee·noh·nee·soh meh tohn THee·kee·ghoh·roh moo*
to make a phone call	**να κάνω ένα τηλέφωνο** *nah kah·noh eh·nah tee·leh·foh·noh*
I'm innocent.	**Είμαι αθώος m /αθώα f.** *ee·meh ah·thoh·ohs/ ah·thoh·ah*

Crime & Lost Property

I want to report...	**Θέλω να αναφέρω...** *theh·loh nah ah nah·feh·roh...*
a mugging	**μια ληστεία** *miah lehs·tee·ah*
a rape	**έναν βιασμό** *eh·nahn vee·ahs·moh*
a theft	**μια κλοπή** *miah kloh·pee*
I've been robbed/ mugged.	**Με έκλεψαν/λήστεψαν.** *meh ehk·leh·psahn/ lees·teh·psahn*
My...has/have been stolen.	**Μου έκλεψαν...μου.** *moo ehk·leh·psahn...moo*

I've lost my…	**Έχασα…** _eh·khah·sah_…
knapsack	**τον σάκκο** _tohn sah·koh_
bicycle	**το ποδήλατο** _toh poh·THee·lah·toh_
camera	**τη φωτογραφική μηχανή** _tee foh·tohgh·rah·fee·kee mee·khah·nee_
car	**το αυτοκίνητο ι** _toh ahf·toh·kee·nee·toh_
computer	**τον υπολογιστή** _tohn ee·poh·loh·yees·tee_
credit cards	**τις πιστωτικές κάρτες** _tees pees·toh·tee·kehs kahr·tehs_
jewelry	**τα κοσμήματα** _tah kohs·mee·mah·tah_
money	**τα χρήματα** _tah khree·mah·tah_
passport	**το διαβατήριο** _toh THiah·vah·tee·ree·oh_
purse	**την τσάντα** _teen tsahn·dah_
traveler's checks	**τις ταξιδιωτικές επιταγές** _tees tah·ksee·THee·oh·tee·kehs eh·pee·tah·yehs_
wallet	**το πορτοφόλι** _toh pohr·toh·foh·lee_
I need a police report.	**Θέλω να κάνω αναφορά στην αστυνομία.** _theh·loh nah kah·noh ah·nah·foh·rah steen ah·stee·noh·mee·ah_
Where is the British/American/Irish embassy?	**Πού είναι η αγγλική/αμερικάνικη/ιρλανδική πρεσβεία;** _poo ee·neh ee ag·lee·kee/ah·meh·ree·kah·nee·kee/eer·lahn·THee·kee preh·svee·ah_

Gynecologist

I have menstrual cramps/a vaginal infection.	**Έχω πόνους περιόδου/κολπική μόλυνση.** *eh-khoh poh-noos peh-ree-oh-THoo/kohl-pee-kee moh-leen-see*
I missed my period.	**Έχω καθυστέρηση.** *eh-khoh kah-thees-teh-ree-see*
I'm on the Pill.	**Παίρνω αντισυλληπτικό χάπι.** *pehr-noh ahn-dee-see-leep-tee-koh khah-pee*
I'm (…months) pregnant.	**Είμαι (…μηνών) έγκυος.** *ee-meh (…mee-nohn) eh-gee-ohs*
I'm (not) pregnant.	**(Δεν) Είμαι έγκυος.** *(THehn) ee-meh ehn-gee-ohs*
I haven't had my period for…months.	**Δεν έχω περίοδο εδώ και…μήνες.** *THehn eh-khoh peh-ree-oh-THoh eh-THoh keh…mee-nehs*

For Numbers, see page 156.

Optician

I've lost…	**Έχασα…** *eh-khah-sah…*
a contact lens	**έναν φακό επαφής** *eh-nahn fah-koh eh-pah-fees*
my glasses	**τα γυαλιά μου** *tah yah-lee-ah moo*
a lens	**έναν φακό** *eh-nahn fah-koh*

Payment & Insurance

How much?	**Πόσο;** *poh-soh*
Can I pay by credit card?	**Μπορώ να πληρώσω με αυτή την πιστωτική κάρτα;** *boh-roh nah plee-roh-soh meh ahf-tee teen pees-toh-tee-kee kahr-tah*
I have insurance.	**Έχω ασφάλεια.** *eh-khoh ahs-fah-lee-ah*
Can I have a receipt for my insurance?	**Μπορώ να έχω μια απόδειξη για την ασφάλεια υγείας μου;** *boh-roh nah eh-khoh miah ah-poh-THeek-see yah teen ahs-fah-lee-ah ee-yee-ahs moo*

Pharmacy

ESSENTIAL

Where's the nearest pharmacy?	**Πού είναι το κοντινότερο φαρμακείο;** *poo ee•neh toh kohn•dee•noh•teh•roh fahr•mah•kee•oh*
What time does the pharmacy [chemist] open/close?	**Τι ώρα ανοίγει/κλείνει το φαρμακείο;** *tee oh•rah ah•nee•yee/klee•nee toh fahr•mah•kee•oh*
What would you recommend for...?	**Τι συνιστάτε για...;** *tee see•nees•tah•teh yah...*
How much should I take?	**Πόσο πρέπει να πάρω;** *poh•soh preh•pee nah pah•roh*
Can you fill [make up] this prescription for me?	**Μπορείτε να μου φτιάξετε αυτή τη συνταγή;** *boh•ree•teh nah moo ftiah•kseh•teh ahf•tee tee seen•dah•yee*
I'm allergic to...	**Είμαι αλλεργικός m /αλλεργική f σε** ... *ee•meh ah•lehr•yeek•ohs/ah•lehr•yeek•ee seh...*

Many medications that are prescription-only in other countries can be bought over the counter in Greece. Pharmacies are open during normal working hours and on a rotating basis at all other times, so that there will always be one open 24 hours a day in any given area. Read the list on display in all pharmacy windows to find the one nearest to you.

We are	**Εμείς είμαστε** eh·_mees_ _eem_·ah·steh
You are	**Εσείς είστε** eh·_sees_ ee·steh
They are	**Αυτοί είναι** ahf·_tee_ ee·neh

Αφήνω (to let)	Present
I let	**Εγώ αφήνω** ah·_fee_·noh
You let	**Εσύ αφήνεις** ah·_fee_·nees
He lets	**Αυτός αφήνει** ah·_fee_·nee
She lets	**Αυτή αφήνει** ah·_fee_·nee
We let	**Εμείς αφήνουμε** ah·_fee_·noo·meh
You let	**Εσείς αφήνετε** ah·_fee_·neh·teh
They let	**Αυτοί αφήνουν** ah·_fee_·noon

Φέρνω (to bring)	Present
I bring	**Εγώ φέρνω** _fehr_·noh
You bring	**Εσύ φέρνεις** _fehr_·nees
He brings	**Αυτός φέρνει** _feh_·rnee
She brings	**Αυτή φέρνει** _fehr_·nee
We bring	**Εμείς φέρνουμε** _feh_·rnoo·meh
You bring	**Εσείς φέρνετε** _feh_·neh·teh
They bring	**Αυτοί φέρνουν** _feh_·noon

The infinitive/first person of most Greek verbs end in **ω**:

| to do | **κάνω** _kah_·noh |

To conjugate this verb, drop the final **ω**, and add the appropriate ending:

Κάνω (to do)	Present
I do	**Εγώ κάνω** eh·_goh_ _kahn_·oh
You do	**Εσύ κάνεις** eh·_see_ _kahn_·ees
(familiar or sing.)	
He does	**Αυτός κάνει** ahf·_tohs_ _kahn_·ee
She does	**Αυτή κάνει** ahf·_tee_ _kahn_·ee

We do	**Εμείς κάνουμε** *eh·mees kahn·oo·meh*
You do (form., pl.)	**Εσείς κάνετε** *eh·sees kahn·eh·teh*
They do	**Αυτοί κάνουν** *ahf·tee kahn·oun*

So, by applying this rule you can conjugate another verb ending in **ω**:

Γράφω (to write)	Present
I write	**Εγώ γράφω** *eh·goh grahf·oh*
You write	**Εσύ γράφεις** *eh·see grahf·ees*
He writes	**Αυτός γράφει** *ahf·tohs grahf·ee*
She writes	**Αυτή γράφει** *ahf·tee grahf·ee*
We write	**Εμείς γράφουμε** *eh·mees grahf·oo·meh*
You write	**Εσείς γράφετε** *eh·sees grahf·eh·teh*
They write	**Αυτοί γράφουν** *ahf·ee grahf·oon*

Word Order

Syntax in Greek, especially in everyday spoken language, is very flexible. The standard word order is subject-verb-object, but you can change the order of sentence components to shift emphasis.

Example:

Το τρένο φεύγει τώρα. *toh treh·noh fehv·ghee toh·rah*

The train leaves now.

You can say the same thing by placing the verb at the beginning of the sentence:

Φεύγει το τρένο τώρα. *fehv·ghee toh treh·noh toh·rah*

The train leaves now.

Also, use an interrogatory intonation to turn this sentence into a question. The question form can work both with the verb in the beginning and at the end of the sentence.

Τώρα φεύγει το τραίνο; *toh·rah fehv·ghee toh treh·noh*

Is the train leaving now?

Note that, in Greek, the equivalent of a semi-colon (;) is used in place of a question mark.

Negation

To form a negative sentence in Greek, add the word **δεν** (*THehn*) before the verb.

Example:

Θέλω <u>theh</u>·loh	I want
Δεν θέλω *THehn* <u>theh</u>·loh	I don't want

Imperatives

Imperative sentences are formed by adding the appropriate ending to the stem of the verb. The endings used to form the imperative of a verb are mainly:
α (*ah*), **ε** (*eh*), **ήσου** (<u>ee</u>·soo), **άσου** (<u>ah</u>·soo).

Examples:	**πηγαίνω** pee·<u>yeh</u>·noh	to go
	Πήγαινε! <u>pee</u>·yeh·neh	Go!
	βιάζομαι <u>viah</u>·zoh·meh	to hurry
	Βιάσου! <u>viah</u>·soo	Hurry!

Nouns & Articles

There are three genders in Greek: masculine, feminine and neuter; all nouns in Greek are assigned a specific gender. The gender of the article changes based on the gender of the noun it modifies. For example:

She is tall.	**Είναι ψηλή.** <u>ee</u>·neh psee·<u>lee</u>
He is tall.	**Είναι ψηλός.** <u>ee</u>·neh psee·<u>lohs</u>

The article **o** (oh) is used with masculine nouns, **η** (ee) with feminine nouns and **το** (toh) with neuter nouns.

masculine	**ο καφές** oh kah·<u>fehs</u>	the coffee
feminine	**η μπίρα** ee <u>bee</u>·rah	the beer
neuter	**το τρένο** toh <u>treh</u>·noh	the train

Greek nouns have four cases: nominative, genitive, accusative and vocative. A simple way to explain their use would be that the nominative indicates the subject, the genitive indicates possession, the accusative indicates the object and the vocative is used to address someone. Don't worry too much about this. In most cases, people will understand what you are saying even if you use a noun with the wrong case. The words in the dictionary are in nominative. There is no easy way to form the plural. Beginner speakers of Greek should clearly state the number along with the noun to be easily understood.

Adjectives

Adjectives agree with the noun they describe in gender, case and number. The most common ending for a feminine adjective is **–η** *(ee)*, for a masculine adjective it is **–ος** *(ohs)* and for the neuter **o** *(oh)*.
Example:

Είναι γρήγορος οδηγός.   *ee·neh ghree·ghoh·rohs oh·THee·ghohs*
He is a fast driver.

Είναι γρήγορη οδηγός.   *ee·neh ghree·ghoh·ree oh·THee·ghohs*
She is a fast driver.

Είναι γρήγορο αυτοκίνητο.   *ee·neh ghree·ghoh·roh ah·ftoh·kee·nee·toh*
This is a fast car.

Comparatives & Superlatives

The comparative form of adjectives is usually formed by adding the word **πιο** *(pioh)* before the adjective. Also, in certain cases, the comparative may be formed by adding the ending **–ερος** *m (eh·rohs)*, **–ερη** *f (eh·ree)*, **–ερο** *(eh·roh)* *n* to the stem of an adjective, respectively. To form the superlative of an adjective, add the ending **–ατος** *m (ah·tohs)*, **–ατη** *f (ah·tee)*, **–ατο** *(ah·tee)* *(n* to the stem of the adjective.

Possessive Pronouns

mine	**μου** *moo*	
yours	**σου** *soo*	
his/her/its	**του/της/του** *too/tees/too*	
ours	**μας** *mahs*	
yours	**σας** *sahs*	
theirs	**τους** *toos*	

| twice | **δύο φορές** _THee_·oh foh·_rehs_ |
| three times | **τρεις φορές** trees foh·_rehs_ |

Time

ESSENTIAL

What time is it?	**Τι ώρα είναι;** tee _oh_·rah ee·neh
It's noon [midday].	**Είναι μεσημέρι.** _ee_·neh meh·see·_meh_·ree
At midnight.	**Τα μεσάνυχτα.** tah meh·_sah_·neekh·tah
From nine o'clock.	**Από τις εννέα ως τις πέντε.** ah·_poh_ tees
to five o'clock	eh·_neh_·ah ohs tees _pehn_·deh
Twenty after [past]	**Τέσσερις και είκοσι.** _teh_·seh·rees keh _ee_·koh·see
four.	
A quarter to nine.	**Εννέα παρά τέταρτο.** eh·_neh_·ah pah·_rah_
	teh·tahr·toh
5:30 a.m./p.m.	**Πεντέμιση π.μ./μ.μ.** pehn·_deh_·mee·see
	proh meh·seem·_vree_·ahs/meh·_tah_ meh·seem·_vree_·ahs

Days

ESSENTIAL

Monday	**Δευτέρα** THehf·_teh_·rah
Tuesday	**Τρίτη** _tree_·tee
Wednesday	**Τετάρτη** teh·_tahr_·tee
Thursday	**Πέμπτη** _pehm_·tee
Friday	**Παρασκευή** pah·rahs·keh·_vee_
Saturday	**Σάββατο** _sah_·vah·toh
Sunday	**Κυριακή** keer·yah·_kee_

Dates

yesterday	**χτες**	*khtehs*
today	**σήμερα**	<u>see</u>·meh·rah
tomorrow	**αύριο**	<u>ahv</u>·ree·oh
day	**ημέρα**	ee·<u>meh</u>·rah
week	**εβδομάδα**	ehv·THoh·<u>mah</u>·THah
month	**μήνας**	<u>mee</u>·nahs
year	**χρόνος**	<u>khroh</u>·nohs

Greece follows a day-month-year format instead of the month-day-year format used in the U.S.
E.g.: July 25, 2008; 25/07/08 = 7/25/2008 in the U.S.

Months

January	**Ιανουάριος**	ee·ah·noo·<u>ah</u>·ree·ohs
February	**Φεβρουάριος**	fehv·roo·<u>ah</u>·ree·ohs
March	**Μάρτιος**	<u>mahr</u>·tee·ohs
April	**Απρίλιος**	ahp·<u>ree</u>·lee·ohs
May	**Μάιος**	<u>mah</u>·ee·ohs
June	**Ιούνιος**	ee·<u>oo</u>·nee·ohs
July	**Ιούλιος**	ee·<u>oo</u>·lee·ohs
August	**Αύγουστος**	<u>ahv</u>·ghoo·stohs
September	**Σεπτέμβριος**	sehp·<u>tehm</u>·vree·ohs
October	**Οκτώβριος**	ohk·<u>toh</u>·vree·ohs
November	**Νοέμβριος**	noh·<u>ehm</u>·vree·ohs
December	**Δεκέμβριος**	THeh·<u>kehm</u>·vree·ohs

Seasons

spring	**η άνοιξη**	ee <u>ah</u>·nee·ksee
summer	**το καλοκαίρι**	toh kah·loh·<u>keh</u>·ree
fall [autumn]	**το φθινόπωρο**	toh fthee·<u>noh</u>·poh·roh
winter	**ο χειμώνας**	oh khee·<u>moh</u>·nahs

trah·<u>peh</u>·zees
bank loan τραπεζικό δάνειο
  trah·peh·zee·<u>koh</u> <u>THah</u>·nee·oh
bar μπαρ bahr
barber κουρείο koo·<u>ree</u>·oh
basket καλάθι kah·<u>lah</u>·THee
basketball μπάσκετ <u>bah</u>·skeht
bathing suit μαγιό mah·<u>yoh</u>
bathroom μπάνιο <u>bah</u>·nioh
battery μπαταρία bah·tah·<u>ree</u>·ah
beach παραλία pah·rah·<u>lee</u>·ah
beautiful όμορφος <u>oh</u>·mohr·fohs
bed κρεβάτι kreh·<u>vah</u>·tee
bed and breakfast διαμονή με
  πρωινό THiah·moh·<u>nee</u> meh
  proh·ee·<u>noh</u>
bedding σεντόνια sehn·<u>doh</u>·niah
bedroom υπνοδωμάτιο
  eep·noh·THoh·<u>mah</u>·tee·oh
before πριν preen
beginner αρχάριος ahr·<u>khah</u>·ree·ohs
belong ανήκω ah·<u>nee</u>·koh
belt ζώνη <u>zoh</u>·nee
bicycle ποδήλατο poh·<u>THee</u>·lah·toh
big μεγάλος meh·<u>ghah</u>·lohs
bikini μπικίνι bee·<u>kee</u>·nee
bird πουλί poo·<u>lee</u>
bite n (insect) **τσίμπημα**
  <u>tsee</u>·bee·mah
bladder ουροδόχος κύστη
  oo·roh·<u>THoh</u>·khohs <u>kee</u>·stee
blanket κουβέρτα koo·<u>veh</u>·rtah
bleed n **αιμορραγία**
  eh·moh·rah·<u>yee</u>·ah; v **αιμορραγώ**

eh·moh·rah·<u>yoh</u>
blinds περσίδες peh·<u>rsee</u>·THehs
blister φουσκάλα foo·<u>skah</u>·lah
blood αίμα <u>eh</u>·mah
blood group ομάδα αίματος
  oh·<u>mah</u>·THah <u>eh</u>·mah·tohs
blood pressure πίεση <u>pee</u>·eh·see
blouse μπλούζα <u>bloo</u>·zah
boarding card κάρτα επιβίβασης
  <u>kah</u>·rtah eh·pee·<u>vee</u>·vah·sees
boat βάρκα <u>vahr</u>·kah
boat trip ταξίδι με πλοίο
  tah·<u>ksee</u>·THee meh <u>plee</u>·oh
body σώμα <u>soh</u>·mah
bone οστό oh·<u>stoh</u>
book n **βιβλίο** veev·<u>lee</u>·oh; v **κάνω**
  κράτηση <u>kah</u>·noh <u>krah</u>·tee·see
bookstore βιβλιοπωλείο
  veev·lee·oh·poh·<u>lee</u>·oh
boot μπότα <u>boh</u>·tah
border (country) **σύνορο** <u>see</u>·noh·roh
boring βαρετός vah·reh·<u>tohs</u>
borrow δανείζομαι
  THah·<u>nee</u>·zoh·meh
botanical garden βοτανικός κήπος
  voh·tah·nee·<u>kohs</u> <u>kee</u>·pohs
bottle μπουκάλι boo·<u>kah</u>·lee
bottle opener τιρμπουσόν
  teer·boo·<u>sohn</u>
bowel έντερο <u>ehn</u>·deh·roh
box office ταχυδρομική θυρίδα
  tah·khee·THroh·mee·<u>kee</u>
  THee·<u>ree</u>·THah
boxing n **μποξ** bohks

boy αγόρι ah·<u>ghoh</u>·ree
boyfriend φίλος <u>fee</u>·lohs
bra σουτιέν soo·<u>tiehn</u>
break n **διάλειμμα** THee·<u>ah</u>·lee·mah;
  v **σπάω** <u>spah</u>·oh
breakdown n (car) **βλάβη** <u>vlah</u>·vee
breakfast πρωινό proh·ee·<u>noh</u>
break-in n **διάρρηξη**
  THee·<u>ah</u>·ree·ksee
breast στήθος <u>stee</u>·THohs
breathe αναπνέω ah·nahp·<u>neh</u>·oh
breathtaking φαντασμαγορικός
  fahn·dahz·mah·ghoh·ree·<u>kohs</u>
bridge n (over water) **γέφυρα**
  <u>yeh</u>·fee·rah; (card game) **μπριτζ**
  breetz
briefcase χαρτοφύλακας
  khah·rtoh·<u>fee</u>·lah·kahs
briefs (men's, women's) **σλιπ**
  sleep (women's); **κυλοτάκι**
  kee·loh·<u>tah</u>·kee
bring φέρνω <u>fehr</u>·noh
Britain Βρετανία vreh·tah·<u>nee</u>·ah
British adj **βρετανικός**
  vreh·tah·nee·<u>kohs</u>; (nationality)
  Βρετανός vreh·tah·<u>nohs</u>
brochure φυλλάδιο fee·<u>lah</u>·THee·oh
broken σπασμένος spahz·<u>meh</u>·nohs
broom n **σκούπα** <u>skoo</u>·pah
browse ξεφυλλίζω kseh·fee·<u>lee</u>·zoh
bruise n **μελανιά** meh·lah·<u>niah</u>
brush n **βούρτσα** <u>voor</u>·tsah; v
  βουρτσίζω voor·<u>tsee</u>·zoh
build κτίζω <u>ktee</u>·zoh

building κτίριο <u>ktee</u>·ree·oh
burn n **έγκαυμα** <u>eh</u>·gahv·mah
bus λεωφορείο leh·oh·foh·<u>ree</u>·oh
bus route διαδρομή λεωφορείων
  THee·ah·THroh·<u>mee</u>
  leh·oh·foh·<u>ree</u>·ohn
bus station σταθμός λεωφορείων
  stahTH·<u>mohs</u> leh·oh·foh·<u>ree</u>·ohn
bus stop στάση λεωφορείου
  <u>stah</u>·see leh·oh·foh·<u>ree</u>·oo
business class μπίζνες θέση
  <u>bee</u>·znehs <u>theh</u>·see
business trip επαγγελματικό
  ταξίδι eh·pah·gehl·mah·tee·<u>koh</u>
  tah·<u>ksee</u>·THee
busy (occupied) **απασχολημένος**
  ah·pahs·khoh·lee·<u>meh</u>·nohs
but αλλά ah·<u>lah</u>
butane gas υγραέριο
  eegh·rah·<u>eh</u>·ree·oh
butcher shop κρεοπωλείο
  kreh·oh·poh·<u>lee</u>·oh
button κουμπί koo·<u>bee</u>
buy αγοράζω ah·ghoh·<u>rah</u>·zoh

C

cabaret καμπαρέ kah·bah·<u>reh</u>
cabin καμπίνα kah·<u>bee</u>·nah
cable car τελεφερίκ teh·leh·feh·<u>reek</u>
cafe καφετέρια kah·feh·<u>teh</u>·ree·ah
calendar ημερολόγιο
  ee·meh·roh·<u>loh</u>·yee·oh
call collect με χρέωση του
  καλούμενου meh <u>khreh</u>·oh·see too

courier *n* (messenger) **κούριερ**
koo•ree•ehr

court house δικαστήριο
THee•kahs•tee•ree•oh

cramp *n* **κράμπα** krahm•bah

credit card πιστωτική κάρτα
pees•toh•tee•kee kahr•tah

crib [cot BE] παιδικό κρεβάτι
peh•THee•koh kreh•vah•tee

crown *n* (dental, royal) **κορώνα**
koh•roh•nah

cruise *n* **κρουαζιέρα** kroo•ahz•yeh•rah

crutch *n* (walking support) **δεκανίκι**
THeh•kah•nee•kee

crystal *n* **κρύσταλλο** kree•stah•loh

cup φλυτζάνι flee•jah•nee

cupboard ντουλάπα doo•lah•pah

currency νόμισμα noh•meez•mah

**currency exchange office γραφείο
ανταλλαγής συναλλάγματος**
ghrah•fee•oh ahn•dah•lah•yees
see•nah•lahgh•mah•tohs

customs (tolls) τελωνείο
teh•loh•nee•oh

**customs declaration (tolls)
τελωνειακή δήλωση**
teh•loh•nee•ah•kee THee•loh•see

cut *n* (wound) **κόψιμο** koh•psee•moh

cut glass *n* **σκαλιστό γυαλί**
skah•lees•toh yah•lee

cycle helmet κράνος ποδηλάτη
krah•nohs poh•THee•lah•tee

cyclist ποδηλάτης poh•THee•lah•tees

Cypriot *adj* **κυπριακός**

keep•ree•ah•kohs; (nationality)
Κύπριος kee•pree•ohs

Cyprus Κύπρος kee•prohs

D

damage *n* **ζημιά** zee•miah; *v*
καταστρέφω kah•tah•streh•foh

dance *v* **χορεύω** khoh•reh•voh

dangerous επικίνδυνος
eh•pee•keen•THee•nohs

dark *adj* (color) **σκούρος** skoo•rohs

dawn *n* **ξημερώματα**
ksee•meh•roh•mah•tah

day trip ημερήσια εκδρομή
ee•meh•ree•see•ah ehk•THroh•mee

deaf κουφός koo•fohs

decide αποφασίζω
ah•poh•fah•see•zoh

deck *n* **κατάστρωμα**
kah•tah•stroh•mah

deck chair σεζ-λονγκ sehz lohng

declare δηλώνω THee•loh•noh

deduct (money) **αφαιρώ** ah•feh•roh

defrost ξεπαγώνω
kseh•pah•ghoh•noh

degrees (temperature) βαθμοί
vahth•mee

delay *n* **καθυστέρηση**
kah•thee•steh•ree•see; *v* **καθυστερώ**
kah•thee•steh•roh

delicious νόστιμος nohs•tee•mohs

deliver παραδίδω
pah•rah•THee•THoh

dental floss οδοντικό νήμα

oh·THohn·dee·<u>koh</u> nee·mah

dentist οδοντίατρος
oh·THohn·<u>dee</u>·ah·trohs

deodorant αποσμητικό
ah·pohz·mee·tee·<u>koh</u>

department store πολυκατάστημα
poh·lee·kah·<u>tahs</u>·tee·mah

departure (travel) αναχώρηση
ah·nah·<u>khoh</u>·ree·see

departure lounge αίθουσα
αναχωρήσεων <u>eh</u>·thoo·sah
ah·nah·khoh·<u>ree</u>·seh·ohn

depend εξαρτώμαι eh·ksahr·<u>toh</u>·meh

deposit n (down payment)
προκαταβολή proh·kah·tah·voh·<u>lee</u>

describe περιγράφω
peh·reegh·<u>rah</u>·foh

designer σχεδιαστής
skheh·THee·ahs·<u>tees</u>

detergent απορρυπαντικό
ah·poh·ree·pahn·dee·<u>koh</u>

develop (photos) εμφανίζω
ehm·fah·<u>nee</u>·zoh

diabetes διαβήτης THee·ah·<u>vee</u>·tees

diabetic διαβητικός
THee·ah·vee·tee·<u>kohs</u>

diagnosis διάγνωση
THee·<u>ahgh</u>·noh·see

dialing code κωδικός koh·THee·<u>kohs</u>

diamond n διαμάντι THiah·<u>mahn</u>·dee

diaper πάνα μωρού <u>pah</u>·nah moh·<u>roo</u>

diarrhea διάρροια THee·<u>ah</u>·ree·ah

dice n ζάρια <u>zah</u>·riah

dictionary λεξικό leh·ksee·<u>koh</u>

diesel ντήζελ <u>dee</u>·zehl

diet n δίαιτα <u>THee</u>·eh·tah

difficult δύσκολος <u>THee</u>·skoh·lohs

dining room τραπεζαρία
trah·peh·zah·<u>ree</u>·ah

dinner βραδινό vrah·THee·<u>noh</u>

direct v κατευθύνω
kah·tehf·<u>thee</u>·noh

direction n (instruction) οδηγία
oh·THee·<u>yee</u>·ah

dirty adj βρώμικος <u>vroh</u>·mee·kohs

disabled άτομο με ειδικές ανάγκες
<u>ah</u>·toh·moh meh ee· ·<u>nahn</u>
THee·<u>kehs</u> ah ·gehs

discounted ticket μειωμένο
εισιτήριο mee·oh·<u>meh</u>·noh
ee·see·<u>tee</u>·ree·oh

dishwashing liquid λίγο υγρό
πιάτων <u>lee</u>·ghoh ee·<u>ghroh</u> piah·tohn

district περιφέρεια
peh·ree·<u>feh</u>·ree·ah

disturb ενοχλώ eh·noh·<u>khloh</u>

diving equipment καταδυτικός
εξοπλισμός kah·tah·THee·tee·<u>kohs</u>
eh·ksoh·pleez·<u>mohs</u>

divorced διαζευγμένος
THee·ah·zehv·<u>ghmeh</u>·nohs

dock προκυμαία proh·kee·<u>meh</u>·ah

doctor γιατρός yah·<u>trohs</u>

doll κούκλα <u>kook</u>·lah

dollar δολάριο THoh·<u>lah</u>·ree·oh

door πόρτα <u>pohr</u>·tah

dosage δοσολογία
THoh·soh·loh·<u>yee</u>·ah

festival φεστιβάλ fehs·tee·<u>vahl</u>
fever πυρετός pee·reh·<u>tohs</u>
fiancé αρραβωνιαστικός
  ah·rah·voh·niahs·tee·<u>kohs</u>
fiancée αρραβωνιαστικιά
  ah·rah·voh·niahs·tee·<u>kiah</u>
filling (dental) σφράγισμα
  <u>sfrah</u>·yeez·mah
film *n* **(camera) φιλμ** feelm
filter *n* **φίλτρο** <u>feel</u>·troh
fine *adv* **καλά** kah·<u>lah</u>; *n* **πρόστιμο**
  <u>prohs</u>·tee·moh
finger *n* **δάχτυλο** <u>THAkh</u>·tee·loh
fire *n* **φωτιά** foh·<u>tiah</u>
fire brigade [BE] πυροσβεστική
  pee·rohz·vehs·tee·<u>kee</u>
fire escape έξοδος κινδύνου
  <u>eh</u>·ksoh·THohs keen·<u>THee</u>·noo
fire extinguisher πυροσβεστήρας
  pee·rohz·vehs·<u>tee</u>·rahs
first class πρώτη θέση <u>proh</u>·tee
  <u>theh</u>·see
first-aid kit κουτί πρώτων
  βοηθειών koo·<u>tee proh</u>·tohn
  voh·ee·thee·<u>ohn</u>
fishing ψάρεμα <u>psah</u>·reh·mah
flag *n* **σημαία** see·<u>meh</u>·ah
flashlight φακός fah·<u>kohs</u>
flat *adj* **επίπεδος** eh·<u>pee</u>·peh·Thohs; *n*
  διαμέρισμα THee·ah·<u>mehr</u>·ees·mah
flea ψύλλος <u>psee</u>·lohs
flight πτήση <u>ptee</u>·see
flight number αριθμός πτήσεως
  ah·reeth·<u>mohs</u> <u>ptee</u>·seh·ohs

flip-flops σαγιονάρες
  sah·yoh·<u>nah</u>·rehs
flood *n* **πλημμύρα** plee·<u>mee</u>·rah
florist ανθοπωλείο
  ahn·thoh·poh·<u>lee</u>·oh
flower *n* **λουλούδι** loo·<u>loo</u>·THee
flu γρίππη <u>ghree</u>·pee
flush τραβώ το καζανάκι trah·<u>voh</u>
  toh kah·zah·<u>nah</u>·kee
fly *n* **μύγα** <u>mee</u>·ghah; *v* **πετάω**
  peh·<u>tah</u>·oh
follow *v* **ακολουθώ** ah·koh·loo·<u>thoh</u>
foot πόδι <u>poh</u>·THee
football [BE] ποδόσφαιρο
  poh·<u>THohs</u>·feh·roh
footpath μονοπάτι moh·noh·<u>pah</u>·tee
forecast *n* **πρόβλεψη** <u>prohv</u>·leh·psee
foreign ξένος <u>kseh</u>·nohs
foreign currency ξένο συνάλλαγμα
  <u>kseh</u>·noh see·<u>nah</u>·lahgh·mah
forest *n* **δάσος** <u>THah</u>·sohs
forget ξεχνώ ksehkh·<u>noh</u>
form *n* **έντυπο** <u>ehn</u>·dee·poh
fortunately ευτυχώς ehf·tee·<u>khohs</u>
forward προωθώ proh·oh·<u>thoh</u>
fountain συντριβάνι
  seen·dree·<u>vah</u>·nee
free *adj* **(available) ελεύθερος**
  eh·<u>lehf</u>·theh·rohs
freezer κατάψυξη kah·<u>tah</u>·psee·ksee
frequent *adj* **συχνός** seekh·<u>nohs</u>
fresh *adj* **φρέσκος** <u>frehs</u>·kohs
friend *n* **φίλος** <u>fee</u>·lohs
frightened φοβισμένος

foh•veez•<u>meh</u>•nohs

from από ah•<u>poh</u>

front *n* **προκυμαία** proh•kee•<u>meh</u>•ah

full *adj* **γεμάτος** yeh•<u>mah</u>•tohs

furniture έπιπλα <u>eh</u>•peep•lah

fuse *n* **ασφάλεια** ahs•<u>fah</u>•lee•ah

G

gambling τζόγος <u>joh</u>•ghohs

game (toy) παιχνίδι pehkh•<u>nee</u>•THee

garage γκαράζ gah•<u>rahz</u>

garden *n* **κήπος** <u>kee</u>•pohs

gas βενζίνη vehn•<u>zee</u>•nee

gas station βενζινάδικο
vehn•zee•<u>nah</u>•THee•koh

gastritis γαστρίτιδα
ghahs•<u>tree</u>•tee•THah

gate (airport) έξοδος <u>eh</u>•ksoh•THohs

genuine αυθεντικός
ahf•thehn•dee•<u>kohs</u>

get off (transport) κατεβαίνω
kah•teh•<u>veh</u>•noh

get out (of vehicle) βγαίνω
<u>vyeh</u>•noh

gift δώρο <u>THoh</u>•roh

**gift store κατάστημα με είδη
δώρων** kah•<u>tahs</u>•tee•mah meh
ee•THee <u>THoh</u>•rohn

girl κορίτσι koh•<u>ree</u>•tsee

girlfriend φίλη <u>fee</u>•lee

give δίνω <u>THee</u>•noh

glass (container) ποτήρι poh•<u>tee</u>•ree

glasses (optical) γυαλιά yah•<u>liah</u>

glove *n* **γάντι** <u>ghahn</u>•dee

go πηγαίνω pee•<u>yeh</u>•noh

gold *n* **χρυσός** khree•<u>sohs</u>

golf γκόλφ gohlf

golf course γήπεδο γκολφ
<u>yee</u>•peh•THoh gohlf

good καλός kah•<u>lohs</u>

grass γρασίδι ghrah•<u>see</u>•THee

gratuity φιλοδώρημα
fee•loh•<u>THoh</u>•ree•mah

greasy (hair, skin) λιπαρός
lee•pah•<u>rohs</u>

Greece Ελλάδα eh•<u>lah</u>•THah

Greek *adj* **ελληνικός** eh•lee•nee•<u>kohs</u>;
(nationality) Έλληνας <u>eh</u>•lee•nahs

greengrocer [BE] οπωροπωλείο
oh•poh•roh•poh•<u>lee</u>•oh

ground (earth) έδαφος <u>eh</u>•THah•fohs

group *n* **γκρουπ** groop

guarantee *n* **εγγύηση** eh•<u>gee</u>•ee•see;
v **εγγυώμαι** eh•gee•<u>oh</u>•meh

guide book τουριστικός οδηγός
too•ree•stee•<u>kohs</u> oh•THee•<u>ghohs</u>

guided tour ξενάγηση
kseh•<u>nah</u>•yee•see

guitar κιθάρα kee•<u>thah</u>•rah

gynecologist γυναικολόγος
yee•neh•koh•<u>loh</u>•ghohs

H

hair μαλλιά mah•<u>liah</u>

hairbrush βούρτσα <u>voor</u>•tsah

hair dresser κομμωτήριο
koh•moh•<u>tee</u>•ree•oh

hair dryer σεσουάρ seh•soo•<u>ahr</u>

half μισός mee·<u>sohs</u>
hammer σφυρί sfee·<u>ree</u>
hand n χέρι <u>kheh</u>·ree
hand luggage αποσκευές χειρός
  ah·pohs·keh·<u>vehs</u> khee·<u>rohs</u>
handbag τσάντα <u>tsahn</u>·dah
handicraft λαϊκή τέχνη lah·ee·<u>kee</u>
  <u>tehkh</u>·nee
handicapped-accessible toilet
  προσβάσιμη τουαλέτα για
  ανάπηρους prohs·<u>vah</u>·see·mee
  too·ah·<u>leh</u>·tah yah ah·<u>nah</u>·pee·roos
handkerchief χαρτομάντηλο
  khah·rtoh·<u>mahn</u>·dee·loh
handle n πόμολο <u>poh</u>·moh·loh
hanger κρεμάστρα kreh·<u>mahs</u>·trah
harbor n λιμάνι lee·<u>mah</u>·nee
hat καπέλο kah·<u>peh</u>·loh
have (possession) έχω <u>eh</u>·khoh
have to (obligation) οφείλω
  oh·<u>fee</u>·loh
head n κεφάλι keh·<u>fah</u>·lee
headache πονοκέφαλος
  poh·noh·<u>keh</u>·fah·lohs
health food store κατάστημα με
  υγιεινές τροφές kah·<u>tahs</u>·tee·mah
  meh ee·yee·ee·<u>nehs</u> troh·<u>fehs</u>
health insurance ασφάλεια υγείας
  ahs·<u>fah</u>·lee·ah ee·<u>yee</u>·ahs
hearing aid ακουστικό βαρυκοΐας
  ah·koo·stee·<u>koh</u> vah·ree·koh·<u>ee</u>·ahs
heart v καρδιά kahr·THee·<u>ah</u>
heart attack καρδιακό έμφραγμα
  kahr·THee·ah·<u>koh</u> <u>ehm</u>·frahgh·mah

heat wave καύσωνας <u>kahf</u>·soh·nahs
heater (water) θερμοσίφωνας
  thehr·moh·<u>see</u>·foh·nahs
heating θέρμανση <u>thehr</u>·mahn·see
heavy βαρύς vah·<u>rees</u>
height ύψος <u>ee</u>·psohs
helicopter ελικόπτερο
  eh·lee·<u>kohp</u>·teh·roh
help n βοήθεια voh·<u>ee</u>·thee·ah; v
  βοηθώ voh·ee·<u>thoh</u>
here εδώ eh·<u>THoh</u>
highway εθνική οδός ehth·nee·<u>kee</u>
  oh·<u>THohs</u>
hike v κάνω πεζοπορία <u>kah</u>·noh
  peh·zoh·poh·<u>ree</u>·ah
hill λόφος <u>loh</u>·fohs
hire [BE] v νοικιάζω nee·<u>kiah</u>·zoh
history ιστορία ee·stoh·<u>ree</u>·ah
hitchhiking οτοστόπ oh·toh·<u>stohp</u>
hobby (pastime) χόμπυ <u>khoh</u>·bee
hold on περιμένω peh·ree·<u>meh</u>·noh
hole (in clothes) τρύπα <u>tree</u>·pah
holiday [BE] διακοπές
  THee·ah·koh·<u>pehs</u>
honeymoon μήνας του μέλιτος
  <u>mee</u>·nahs too <u>meh</u>·lee·tohs
horse track ιπποδρόμιο
  ee·poh·<u>THroh</u>·mee·oh
hospital νοσοκομείο
  noh·soh·koh·<u>mee</u>·oh
hot (weather) ζεστός zehs·<u>tohs</u>
hot spring θερμή πηγή thehr·<u>mee</u>
  pee·<u>yee</u>
hotel ξενοδοχείο

kseh·noh·THoh·<u>khee</u>·oh

household articles **είδη οικιακής**
χρήσεως ee·THee ee·kee·ah·<u>kees</u>
khree·seh·ohs

husband σύζυγος <u>see</u>·zee·ghohs

I

ice *n* **πάγος** <u>pah</u>·ghohs

identification ταυτότητα
tahf·<u>toh</u>·tee·tah

illegal παράνομος pah·<u>rah</u>·noh·mohs

illness αρρώστεια ahr·<u>ohs</u>·tee·ah

imitation απομίμηση
ah·poh·<u>mee</u>·mee·see

immediately αμέσως ah·<u>meh</u>·sohs

impressive εντυπωσιακός
ehn·dee·poh·see·ah·<u>kohs</u>

included συμπεριλαμβάνεται
seem·beh·ree·lahm·<u>vah</u>·neh·teh

indigestion δυσπεψία
THehs·peh·<u>psee</u>·ah

indoor εσωτερικός
eh·soh·teh·ree·<u>kohs</u>

indoor pool εσωτερική πισίνα
eh·soh·teh·ree·<u>kee</u> pee·<u>see</u>·nah

inexpensive φτηνός ftee·<u>nohs</u>

infected μολυσμένος
moh·leez·<u>meh</u>·nohs

inflammation φλεγμονή
flegh·moh·<u>nee</u>

information πληροφορίες
plee·roh·foh·<u>ree</u>·ehs

information office γραφείο
πληροφοριών ghrah·<u>fee</u>·oh

plee·roh·foh·ree·<u>ohn</u>

injection ένεση eh·neh·see

injured τραυματισμένος
trahv·mah·teez·<u>meh</u>·nohs

innocent αθώος ah·<u>thoh</u>·ohs

insect bite τσίμπημα από
έντομο <u>tseem</u>·bee·mah ah·<u>poh</u>
ehn·doh·moh

insect repellent εντομοαπωθητικό
ehn·doh·moh·ah·poh·thee·tee·<u>koh</u>

inside μέσα <u>meh</u>·sah

insist επιμένω eh·pee·<u>meh</u>·noh

insomnia αϋπνία ah·eep·<u>nee</u>·ah

instruction οδηγία oh·THee·<u>yee</u>·ah

insulin ινσουλίνη een·soo·<u>lee</u>·nee

insurance ασφάλεια ahs·<u>fah</u>·lee·ah

insurance certificate πιστοποιητικό
ασφάλειας pees·toh·pee·ee·tee·<u>koh</u>
ahs·<u>fah</u>·lee·ahs

insurance claim ασφάλεια
αποζημίωσης ahs·<u>fah</u>·lee·ah
ah·poh·zee·<u>mee</u>·oh·sees

insurance company ασφαλιστική
εταιρία ahs·fah·lees·tee·<u>kee</u>
eh·teh·<u>ree</u>·ah

interest rate επιτόκιο
eh·pee·<u>toh</u>·kee·oh

interesting ενδιαφέρων
ehn·THee·ah·<u>feh</u>·rohn

international διεθνής THee·eth·<u>nees</u>

International Student Card διεθνής
φοιτητική κάρτα THee·ehth·<u>nees</u>
fee·tee·tee·<u>kee</u> kahr·tah

internet ίντερνετ <u>ee</u>·nteh·rnet

internet cafe ίντερνετ καφέ
   ee·nteh·rnet kah·<u>feh</u>
interpreter διερμηνέας
   THee·ehr·mee·<u>neh</u>·ahs
interval διάλειμμα THee·<u>ah</u>·lee·mah
introduce συστήνω see·<u>stee</u>·noh
introductions συστάσεις
   see·<u>stah</u>·sees
invitation πρόσκληση <u>prohs</u>·klee·see
invite v προσκαλώ prohs·kah·<u>loh</u>
iodine ιώδειο ee·<u>oh</u>·THee·oh
iron n σίδερο <u>see</u>·THeh·roh; v
   σιδερώνω see·THeh·<u>roh</u>·noh
itemized bill αναλυτικός
   λογαριασμός ah·nah·lee·tee·<u>kohs</u>
   loh·ghahr·yahz·<u>mohs</u>

J

jacket σακάκι sah·<u>kah</u>·kee
jammed σφηνωμένος
   sfee·noh·<u>meh</u>·nohs
jar n βάζο <u>vah</u>·zoh
jaw σαγόνι sah·<u>ghoh</u>·nee
jeans μπλου-τζην bloo·<u>jeen</u>
jellyfish μέδουσα <u>meh</u>·THoo·sah
jet-ski τζετ-σκι jeht·skee
jeweler κοσμηματοπωλείο
   kohz·mee·mah·toh·poh·<u>lee</u>·oh
job δουλειά THoo·<u>liah</u>
jogging τζόγκινγκ joh·geeng
joke n ανέκδοτο ah·<u>nehk</u>·THoh·toh
journey ταξίδι tah·<u>ksee</u>·THee
junction (intersection) κόμβος
   <u>kohm</u>·vohs

K

keep v κρατώ krah·<u>toh</u>
key n κλειδί klee·<u>THee</u>
key card κάρτα-κλειδί
   <u>kahr</u>·tah·klee·<u>dee</u>
key ring μπρελόκ breh·<u>lohk</u>
kidney νεφρό nehf·<u>roh</u>
kind είδος ee·<u>THohs</u>
king βασιλιάς vah·see·<u>liahs</u>
kiosk περίπτερο peh·<u>ree</u>·pteh·roh
kiss n φιλί fee·<u>lee</u>; v φιλώ fee·<u>loh</u>
kitchen χαρτί κουζίνας khah·<u>rtee</u>
   koo·<u>zee</u>·nahs
knapsack σάκκος <u>sah</u>·kohs
knee γόνατο <u>ghoh</u>·nah·toh
knife μαχαίρι mah·<u>kheh</u>·ree
know γνωρίζω ghnoh·<u>ree</u>·zoh

L

label n ετικέτα eh·tee·<u>keh</u>·tah
ladder σκάλα <u>skah</u>·lah
lake λίμνη <u>leem</u>·nee
lamp λάμπα <u>lahm</u>·bah
land n γη ghee; v προσγειώνομαι
   prohz·yee·<u>oh</u>·noh·meh
language course μάθημα ξένης
   γλώσσας <u>mah</u>·thee·mah <u>kseh</u>·nees
   <u>ghloh</u>·sahs
large adj μεγάλος meh·<u>ghah</u>·lohs
last τελευταίος teh·lehf·<u>teh</u>·ohs
late adv αργά ahr·<u>ghah</u>
laugh v γελώ yeh·<u>loh</u>
laundry facility πλυντήριο
   pleen·<u>dee</u>·ree·oh

lavatory μπάνιο bah·nioh
lawyer δικηγόρος
  THee·kee·<u>ghoh</u>·rohs
laxative καθαρτικό
  kah·thahr·tee·<u>koh</u>
learn μαθαίνω mah·<u>theh</u>·noh
leave v (depart) **φεύγω** <u>fehv</u>·ghoh;
  (let go) **αφήνω** ah·<u>fee</u>·noh
left adj **αριστερός** ah·rees·teh·<u>rohs</u>;
  adv **αριστερά** ah·rees·teh·<u>rah</u>
leg πόδι poh·THee
legal νόμιμος <u>noh</u>·mee·mohs
lend δανείζω THah·<u>nee</u>·zoh
length μήκος <u>mee</u>·kohs
lens φακός fah·<u>kohs</u>
lens cap κάλυμμα φακού
  kah·lee·mah fah·<u>koo</u>
less λιγότερο lee·<u>ghoh</u>·teh·roh
letter γράμμα <u>ghrah</u>·mah
level (even) **επίπεδο**
  eh·<u>pee</u>·peh·THoh
library βιβλιοθήκη
  veev·lee·oh·<u>thee</u>·kee
lie down ξαπλώνω ksah·<u>ploh</u>·noh
life boat ναυαγοσωστική λέμβος
  nah·vah·ghoh·sohs·tee·<u>kee</u>
  <u>lehm</u>·vohs
lifeguard ναυαγοσώστης
  nah·vah·ghoh·<u>sohs</u>·tees
life jacket σωσίβιο soh·<u>see</u>·vee·oh
lift [BE] n (elevator) **ασανσέρ**
  ah·sahn·<u>sehr</u>
lift pass άδεια σκι ah·THee·ah skee
light adj (color) **ανοιχτός**

ah·neekh·<u>tohs</u>; n (electric) **φως** fohs
light bulb λάμπα <u>lahm</u>·bah
lighter adj **ανοιχτότερος**
  ah·neekh·<u>toh</u>·teh·rohs; n
  αναπτήρας ah·nahp·<u>tee</u>·rahs
lighthouse φάρος <u>fah</u>·rohs
lights (car) **φώτα** <u>foh</u>·tah
line n (subway) **γραμμή** ghrah·<u>mee</u>
lips χείλη <u>khee</u>·lee
lipstick κραγιόν krah·<u>yohn</u>
liter λίτρο <u>lee</u>·troh
little μικρός meek·<u>rohs</u>
liver συκώτι see·<u>koh</u>·tee
living room σαλόνι sah·<u>loh</u>·nee
local τοπικός toh·pee·<u>kohs</u>
location (space) **θέση** <u>theh</u>·see
lock n (door) **κλειδαριά**
  klee·THahr·<u>yah</u>; (river, canal)
  φράγμα <u>frahgh</u>·mah; v **κλειδώνω**
  klee·<u>THoh</u>·noh
long adj **μακρύς** mak·<u>rees</u>
long-distance bus υπεραστικό
  λεωφορείο ee·peh·rahs·tee·<u>koh</u>
  leh·oh·foh·<u>ree</u>·oh
long-distance call υπεραστικό
  τηλεφώνημα ee·pehr·ahs·tee·<u>koh</u>
  tee·leh·<u>foh</u>·nee·mah
long-sighted [BE] **πρεσβύωπας**
  prehz·<u>vee</u>·oh·pahs
look v **κοιτάω** kee·<u>tah</u>·oh
look for ψάχνω <u>psahkh</u>·noh
loose (fitting) **φαρδύς** fahr·<u>THees</u>
loss n **απώλεια** ah·<u>poh</u>·lee·ah
lotion λοσιόν loh·<u>siohn</u>

moh·noh·**pah**·tee

nausea ναυτία nahf·**tee**·ah

near *adv* κοντά kohn·**dah**

nearby εδώ κοντά eh·THoh kohn·**dah**

necessary απαραίτητος
ah·pah·**reh**·tee·tohs

necklace κολλιέ koh·**lieh**

need *v* χρειάζομαι khree·**ah**·zoh·meh

neighbor *n* γείτονας **yee**·toh·nahs

nerve νεύρο **nehv**·roh

never ποτέ poh·**teh**

new καινούργιος keh·**noor**·yohs

newspaper εφημερίδα
eh·fee·meh·**ree**·THah

newsstand περίπτερο
peh·**ree**·pteh·roh

next επόμενος eh·**poh**·meh·nohs

next to δίπλα THeep·lah

night νύχτα neekh·tah

night club νυχτερινό κέντρο
neekh·teh·ree·**noh** kehn·droh

noisy θορυβώδης
thoh·ree·**voh**·THees

none *adj* κανένας kah·**neh**·nahs

non-smoking μη καπνίζοντες mee
kap·**nee**·zohn·dehs

north βόρεια **voh**·ree·ah

nose *n* μύτη **mee**·tee

nudist beach παραλία γυμνιστών
pah·rah·**lee**·ah yeem·nees·**tohn**

nurse *n* νοσοκόμα noh·soh·**koh**·mah

O

occupied κατειλημένος

kah·tee·lee·**meh**·nohs

office γραφείο ghrah·**fee**·oh

old *adj* (thing) παλιός pah·**liohs**;
(person) γέρικος **yeh**·ree·kohs

old town παλιά πόλη pah·**liah**
poh·lee

old-fashioned ντεμοντέ
deh·mohn·**deh**

once μια φορά miah foh·**rah**

one-way ticket απλό εισιτήριο
ahp·**loh** ee·see·**tee**·ree·oh

open *adj* ανοιχτός ah·neekh·**tohs**; *v*
ανοίγω ah·**nee**·ghoh

opening hours ώρες λειτουργίας
oh·rehs lee·toor·**yee**·ahs

opera όπερα **oh**·peh·rah

opposite απέναντι ah·**peh**·nahn·dee

optician οφθαλμίατρος
ohf·thahl·**mee**·aht·rohs

orchestra ορχήστρα ohr·**khees**·trah

order *v* παραγγέλνω
pah·rah·**ghel**·noh

organized οργανωμένος
ohr·ghah·noh·**meh**·nohs

others άλλα **ah**·lah

out *adv* έξω **eh**·ksoh

outdoor εξωτερικός
eh·ksoh·teh·ree·**kohs**

outside *adj* έξω **eh**·ksoh

oval οβάλ oh·**vahl**

oven φούρνος **foor**·nohs

over there εκεί eh·**kee**

overnight (package) ένα βράδυ
eh·nah vrah·THee

owe χρωστώ khroh·<u>stoh</u>
owner κάτοχος <u>kah</u>·toh·khohs

P

pacifier πιπίλα pee·<u>pee</u>·lah
pack v (baggage) **φτιάχνω τις
βαλίτσες** ftee·<u>ahkh</u>·noh tees
vah·<u>lee</u>·tsehs
paddling pool [BE] ρηχή πισίνα
ree·<u>khee</u> pee·<u>see</u>·nah
padlock λουκέτο loo·<u>keh</u>·toh
pain n **πόνος** <u>poh</u>·nohs
painkiller **παυσίπονο**
pahf·<u>see</u>·poh·noh
paint v **ζωγραφίζω**
zohgh·rah·<u>fee</u>·zoh
pair ζευγάρι zehv·<u>ghah</u>·ree
pajamas πυτζάμες pee·<u>jah</u>·mehs
palace ανάκτορα ah·<u>nahk</u>·toh·rah
panorama πανόραμα
pah·<u>noh</u>·rah·mah
pants παντελόνι pahn·deh·<u>loh</u>·nee
paper χαρτί khar·<u>tee</u>
paralysis παραλυσία
pah·rah·lee·<u>see</u>·ah
parcel πακέτο pah·<u>keh</u>·toh
parents γονείς ghoh·<u>nees</u>
park n **πάρκο** <u>pahr</u>·koh
parking lot χώρος στάθμευσης
<u>khoh</u>·rohs <u>stahth</u>·mehf·sees
parking meter παρκόμετρο
pahr·<u>koh</u>·meht·roh
party n (social gathering) **πάρτυ**
<u>pah</u>·rtee

pass v **περνώ** pehr·<u>noh</u>
passenger επιβάτης eh·pee·<u>vah</u>·tees
passport διαβατήριο
THiah·vah·<u>tee</u>·ree·oh
pastry store ζαχαροπλαστείο
zah·khah·rohp·lahs·<u>tee</u>·oh
path μονοπάτι moh·noh·<u>pah</u>·tee
pay v **πληρώνω** plee·<u>roh</u>·noh
payment πληρωμή plee·roh·<u>mee</u>
peak n **κορυφή** koh·ree·<u>fee</u>
pearl μαργαριτάρι
mahr·ghah·ree·<u>tah</u>·ree
pebbly (beach) με χαλίκια meh
khah·<u>lee</u>·kiah
pedestrian crossing διάβαση πεζών
THee·<u>ah</u>·vah·see peh·<u>zohn</u>
pedestrian zone πεζόδρομος
peh·<u>zohTH</u>·roh·mohs
pen n **στυλό** stee·<u>loh</u>
per την teen
perhaps ίσως <u>ee</u>·sohs
period (menstrual) περίοδος
peh·<u>ree</u>·oh·THohs; (time)
χρονική περίοδος khroh·nee·<u>kee</u>
peh·<u>ree</u>·oh·Thohs
permit n **άδεια** <u>ah</u>·THee·ah
petrol [BE] βενζίνη vehn·<u>zee</u>·nee
pewter κασσίτερος kah·<u>see</u>·teh·rohs
phone n **τηλέφωνο** tee·<u>leh</u>·foh·noh
phone call τηλεφώνημα
tee·leh·<u>foh</u>·nee·mah
phone card τηλεκάρτα
tee·leh·<u>kahr</u>·tah
photo v **φωτογραφία**

foh·tohgh·rah·<u>fee</u>·ah

photocopier φωτοτυπικό
foh·toh·tee·pee·<u>koh</u>

phrase n **φράση** <u>frah</u>·see

pick up παίρνω <u>pehr</u>·noh

picnic area περιοχή για πικνίκ
peh·ree·oh·<u>khee</u> yah peek·neek

piece τεμάχιο teh·<u>mah</u>·khee·oh

pillow μαξιλάρι mah·ksee·<u>lah</u>·ree

pillow case μαξιλαροθήκη
mah·ksee·lah·roh·<u>thee</u>·kee

pipe (smoking) πίπα <u>pee</u>·pah

piste [BE] μονοπάτι
moh·noh·<u>pah</u>·tee

pizzeria πιτσαρία pee·tsah·<u>ree</u>·ah

plan n **σχέδιο** <u>skheh</u>·THee·oh

plane n **αεροπλάνο**
ah·eh·rohp·<u>lah</u>·noh

plant n **φυτό** fee·<u>toh</u>

plastic wrap διαφανή μεμβράνη
THee·ah·fah·<u>nee</u> mehm·<u>vrah</u>·nee

platform αποβάθρα
ah·poh·<u>vahth</u>·rah

platinum πλατίνα plah·<u>tee</u>·nah

play v **(games) παίζω** <u>peh</u>·zoh;
(music) **παίζω** <u>peh</u>·zoh

playground παιδική χαρά
peh·THee·<u>kee</u> khah·<u>rah</u>

pleasant ευχάριστος
ehf·<u>khah</u>·rees·tohs

plug n **πρίζα** <u>pree</u>·zah

point n **σημείο** see·<u>mee</u>·oh; v **δείχνω**
<u>THeekh</u>·noh

poison n **δηλητήριο**

THee·lee·<u>tee</u>·ree·oh

poisonous δηλητηριώδης
THee·lee·tee·ree·<u>oh</u>·THees

police n **αστυνομία**
ah·stee·noh·<u>mee</u>·ah

police station αστυνομικό τμήμα
ah·stee·noh·mee·<u>koh</u> tmee·mah

pond n **λιμνούλα** leem·<u>noo</u>·lah

popular δημοφιλής
THee·moh·fee·<u>lees</u>

porter αχθοφόρος
ahkh·thoh·<u>foh</u>·rohs

portion n **μερίδα** meh·<u>ree</u>·THah

possible πιθανός pee·thah·<u>nohs</u>

postbox [BE] ταχυδρομικό κουτί
tah·kheeTH·roh·mee·<u>koh</u> koo·tee

post card καρτποστάλ
kahrt·poh·<u>stahl</u>

post office ταχυδρομείο
tah·kheeTH·roh·<u>mee</u>·oh

pottery αγγειοπλαστική
ahn·gee·ohp·lahs·tee·<u>kee</u>

pound (sterling) λίρα <u>lee</u>·rah

pregnant έγκυος <u>eh</u>·gee·ohs

prescribe συνταγογραφώ
seen·dah·ghoh·ghrah·<u>foh</u>

prescription συνταγή γιατρού
seen·dah·<u>yee</u> yaht·<u>roo</u>

present δώρο <u>THoh</u>·roh

press v **σιδερώνω** see·TΗeh·<u>roh</u>·noh

pretty adj **όμορφος** <u>oh</u>·mohr·fohs

prison n **φυλακή** fee·lah·<u>kee</u>

private bathroom ιδιωτικό μπάνιο
ee·THee·oh·tee·<u>koh</u> <u>bah</u>·nioh

problem πρόβλημα <u>prohv</u>·lee·mah

program *n* πρόγραμμα
<u>prohgh</u>·rah·mah

program of events πρόγραμμα
θεαμάτων <u>proh</u>·ghrah·mah
theh·ah·<u>mah</u>·tohn

prohibited απαγορευμένος
ah·pah·ghoh·rehv·<u>meh</u>·nohs

pronounce προφέρω proh·<u>feh</u>·roh

public δημόσιος THee·<u>moh</u>·see·ohs

public holiday αργία ahr·<u>yee</u>·ah

pump *n* τρόμπα <u>troh</u>·mbah

purpose σκοπός skoh·<u>pohs</u>

put *v* βάζω <u>vah</u>·zoh

Q

quality ποιότητα pee·<u>oh</u>·tee·tah

quantity ποσότητα poh·<u>soh</u>·tee·tah

quarantine *n* καραντίνα
kah·rahn·<u>dee</u>·nah

quarter (quantity) ένα τέταρτο
eh·nah <u>teh</u>·tah·rtoh

quay αποβάθρα ah·poh·<u>vath</u>·rah

question *n* ερώτηση eh·<u>roh</u>·tee·see

queue [BE] *v* περιμένω στην ουρά
peh·ree·<u>meh</u>·noh steen oo·<u>rah</u>

quick γρήγορος <u>ghree</u>·ghoh·rohs

quiet *adj* ήσυχος <u>ee</u>·see·khohs

R

racket (tennis, squash) ρακέτα
rah·<u>keh</u>·tah

radio *n* ραδιόφωνο
rah·THee·<u>oh</u>·foh·noh

railway station [BE]
σιδηροδρομικός σταθμός
see·THee·rohTH·roh·mee·<u>kohs</u>
stahth·<u>mohs</u>

rain *n* βροχή vroh·<u>khee</u>; *v* βρέχει
<u>vreh</u>·khee

raincoat αδιάβροχο
ah·THee·<u>ahv</u>·roh·khoh

rapids ρεύμα ποταμού <u>rehv</u>·mah
poh·tah·<u>moo</u>

rare (unusual) σπάνιος <u>spah</u>·nee·ohs

rash *n* εξάνθημα eh·<u>ksahn</u>·thee·mah

ravine ρεματιά reh·mah·<u>tiah</u>

razor ξυραφάκι ksee·rah·<u>fah</u>·kee

razor blade ξυραφάκι
ksee·rah·<u>fah</u>·kee

ready *adj* έτοιμος eh·<u>tee</u>·mohs

real (genuine) γνήσιος <u>ghee</u>·see·ohs;
(true) αληθινός ah·lee·thee·nohs

receipt απόδειξη ah·<u>poh</u>·THee·ksee

reception (hotel) ρεσεψιόν
reh·seh·<u>psiohn</u>

recommend συστήνω sees·<u>tee</u>·noh

reduction έκπτωση <u>ehk</u>·ptoh·see

refund *n* επιστροφή χρημάτων
eh·pees·troh·<u>fee</u> khree·<u>mah</u>·tohn

region περιοχή peh·ree·oh·<u>khee</u>

registration number αριθμός
κυκλοφορίας ah·reeth·<u>mohs</u>
kee·kloh·foh·<u>ree</u>·ahs

religion θρησκεία three·<u>skee</u>·ah

remember θυμάμαι thee·<u>mah</u>·meh

rent *v* νοικιάζω nee·<u>kiah</u>·zoh

repair *n* επισκευή eh·pee·skeh·<u>vee</u>; *v*

ah·ksee·oh·<u>theh</u>·ah·toh

sightseeing tour ξενάγηση στα αξιοθέατα kseh·<u>nah</u>·yee·see stah ah·ksee·oh·<u>theh</u>·ah·tah

sign (road) σήμα <u>see</u>·mah

silk μετάξι meh·<u>tah</u>·ksee

silver ασήμι ah·<u>see</u>·mee

simple απλός ahp·<u>lohs</u>

single (not married) ελεύθερος eh·<u>lehf</u>·theh·rohs

single room μονόκλινο δωμάτιο moh·<u>noh</u>·klee·noh THoh·<u>mah</u>·tee·oh

single ticket [BE] απλό εισιτήριο ahp·<u>loh</u> ee·see·<u>tee</u>·ree·oh

sink (bathroom) νιπτήρας nee·<u>ptee</u>·rahs

sit κάθομαι <u>kah</u>·thoh·meh

size *n* **μέγεθος** <u>meh</u>·yeh·thohs

skates παγοπέδιλα pah·ghoh·<u>peh</u>·THee·lah

skating rink παγοδρόμιο pah·ghohTH·<u>roh</u>·mee·oh

ski boots μπότες του σκι <u>boh</u>·tehs too skee

ski poles μπαστούνια του σκι bahs·<u>too</u>·niah too skee

ski school σχολή σκι skhoh·<u>lee</u> skee

skiing σκι skee

skin *n* **δέρμα** <u>Thehr</u>·mah

skirt φούστα <u>foo</u>·stah

sleep *v* **κοιμάμαι** kee·<u>mah</u>·meh

sleeping bag υπνόσακκος ee·<u>pnoh</u>·sah·kohs

sleeping car βαγκόν-λι vah·<u>gohn</u>·lee

sleeping pill υπνωτικό χάπι eep·noh·tee·<u>koh</u> khah·pee

slippers παντόφλες pahn·<u>dohf</u>·lehs

slope (ski) πλαγιά plah·<u>yah</u>

slow *adj* **αργός** ahr·<u>ghohs</u>

small μικρός meek·<u>rohs</u>

smell *v* **μυρίζω** mee·<u>ree</u>·zoh

smoke *v* **καπνίζω** kahp·<u>nee</u>·zoh

smoking area περιοχή για καπνίζοντες peh·ree·oh·<u>khee</u> yah kahp·<u>nee</u>·zohn·dehs

snack bar κυλικείο kee·lee·<u>kee</u>·oh

sneakers αθλητικά παπούτσια ath·lee·tee·<u>kah</u> pah·<u>poo</u>·tsiah

snorkeling equipment εξοπλισμό για ελεύθερη κατάδυση eh·ksohp·leez·<u>moh</u> yah eh·<u>lehf</u>·theh·ree kah·<u>tah</u>·THee·see

snow *v* **χιονίζει** khioh·<u>nee</u>·zee

soap *n* **σαπούνι** sah·<u>poo</u>·nee

soccer ποδόσφαιρο poh·<u>THohs</u>·feh·roh

socket πρίζα <u>pree</u>·zah

socks κάλτσες <u>kahl</u>·tsehs

sofa καναπές kah·nah·<u>pehs</u>

sole (shoes) σόλα <u>soh</u>·lah

something κάτι <u>kah</u>·tee

sometimes μερικές φορές meh·ree·<u>kehs</u> foh·<u>rehs</u>

soon σύντομα <u>seen</u>·doh·mah

soother [BE] πιπίλα pee·<u>pee</u>·lah

sore throat πονόλαιμος poh·<u>noh</u>·leh·mohs

sort *n* **είδος** <u>ee</u>·THohs; *v* **διαλέγω**

THiah•<u>leh</u>•ghoh

south *adj* **νότιος** noh•tee•ohs

souvenir σουβενίρ soo•veh•<u>neer</u>

souvenir store κατάστημα σουβενίρ
kah•<u>tahs</u>•tee•mah soo•veh•<u>neer</u>

spa σπα spah

space *n* (area) **χώρος** <u>khoh</u>•rohs

spare (extra) **επιπλέον**
eh•peep•<u>leh</u>•ohn

speak μιλώ mee•<u>loh</u>

special requirement ειδική ανάγκη
ee•THee•<u>kee</u> ah•<u>nahn</u>•gkee

specialist ειδικός ee•THee•<u>kohs</u>

specimen δείγμα <u>THeeg</u>•mah

speed *v* **τρέχω** <u>treh</u>•khoh

spend ξοδεύω ksoh•<u>THeh</u>•voh

spine σπονδυλική στήλη
spohn•THee•lee•<u>kee</u> <u>stee</u>•lee

spoon *n* **κουτάλι** koo•<u>tah</u>•lee

sport αθλητισμός ahth•lee•teez•<u>mohs</u>

sporting goods store κατάστημα
αθλητικών ειδών kah•<u>tahs</u>•tee•mah
ath•lee•tee•<u>kohn</u> ee•<u>THohn</u>

sports massage αθλητικό μασάζ
ahth•lee•tee•<u>koh</u> mah•<u>sahz</u>

sports stadium αθλητικό στάδιο
ahth•lee•tee•<u>koh</u> stah•THee•oh

square τετράγωνος
teht•<u>rah</u>•ghoh•nohs

stadium στάδιο stah•THee•oh

stain *n* **λεκές** leh•<u>kehs</u>

stairs σκάλες <u>skah</u>•lehs

stale μπαγιάτικος bah•<u>yah</u>•tee•kohs

stamp *n* (postage) **γραμματόσημο**

ghrah•mah•<u>toh</u>•see•moh

start *v* **αρχίζω** ahr•<u>khee</u>•zoh

statement (legal) **δήλωση**
<u>THee</u>•loh•see

statue άγαλμα <u>ah</u>•ghahl•mah

stay *v* **μένω** <u>meh</u>•noh

sterilizing solution αποστειρωτικό
διάλυμα ah•pohs•tee•roh•tee•<u>koh</u>
THee•<u>ah</u>•lee•mah

sting *n* (insect) **τσίμπημα**
<u>tsee</u>•bee•mah

stolen κλεμένος kleh•<u>meh</u>•nohs

stomach *n* **στομάχι** stoh•<u>mah</u>•khee

stomachache στομαχόπονος
stoh•mah•<u>khoh</u>•poh•nohs

stop *n* (bus) **στάση** <u>stah</u>•see; *v*
σταματώ stah•mah•<u>toh</u>

store guide [BE] **οδηγός**
καταστήματος oh•THee•<u>ghohs</u>
kah•tahs•<u>tee</u>•mah•tohs

stove κουζίνα koo•<u>zee</u>•nah

straight ahead ευθεία ehf•<u>thee</u>•ah

strange παράξενος
pah•<u>rah</u>•kseh•nohs

straw (drinking) **καλαμάκι**
kah•lah•<u>mah</u>•kee

stream *n* **ρυάκι** ree•<u>ah</u>•kee

street δρόμος <u>THroh</u>•mohs

string *n* (cord) **σπάγγος** <u>spah</u>•gohs

student φοιτητής fee•tee•<u>tees</u>

study *v* **σπουδάζω** spoo•<u>THah</u>•zoh

style *n* **στυλ** steel

subtitled με υπότιτλους meh
ee•<u>poh</u>•teet•loos

subway μετρό meh·<u>troh</u>

subway station σταθμός μετρό
stahth·<u>mohs</u> meh·<u>troh</u>

suggest προτείνω proh·<u>tee</u>·noh

suit (men's) κουστούμι
koos·<u>too</u>·mee; **(women's)** ταγιέρ
tah·<u>yehr</u>

suitable κατάλληλος
kah·<u>tah</u>·lee·lohs

sunburn n έγκαυμα ηλίου
ehn·gahv·mah ee·<u>lee</u>·oo

sunglasses γυαλιά ηλίου yah·<u>liah</u>
ee·<u>lee</u>·oo

sunshade [BE] ομπρέλλα
ohm·<u>breh</u>·lah

sunstroke ηλίαση ee·<u>lee</u>·ah·see

sun tan lotion λοσιόν μαυρίσματος
loh·<u>siohn</u> mahv·<u>rees</u>·mah·tohs

sunscreen αντιηλιακό
ahn·dee·ee·lee·ah·<u>koh</u>

superb έξοχος eh·ksoh·khohs

supermarket σουπερμάρκετ
soo·pehr·<u>mahr</u>·keht

supervision επίβλεψη
eh·<u>peev</u>·leh·psee

surname επίθετο eh·<u>pee</u>·theh·toh

sweatshirt φούτερ <u>foo</u>·tehr

swelling πρήξιμο <u>pree</u>·ksee·moh

swimming κολύμβηση
koh·<u>leem</u>·vee·see

swimming pool πισίνα pee·<u>see</u>·nah

swimming trunks μαγιό mah·<u>yoh</u>

swimsuit μαγιό mah·<u>yoh</u>

switch n διακόπτης THiah·<u>koh</u>·ptees

swollen πρησμένος preez·<u>meh</u>·nohs

symptom σύμπτωμα <u>seem</u>·ptoh·mah

T

table τραπέζι trah·<u>peh</u>·zee

tablecloth τραπεζομάντηλο
trah·peh·zoh·<u>mahn</u>·dee·loh

tablet χάπι <u>khah</u>·pee

take παίρνω <u>pehr</u>·noh

take a photograph βγάζω
φωτογραφία <u>vghah</u>·zoh
foh·tohgh·rah·<u>fee</u>·ah

take away [BE] πακέτο για το σπίτι
pah·<u>keh</u>·toh yah toh <u>spee</u>·tee

tall ψηλός psee·<u>lohs</u>

tampon ταμπόν tahm·<u>bohn</u>

tax n φόρος <u>foh</u>·rohs

taxi ταξί tah·<u>ksee</u>

taxi driver ταξιτζής tah·ksee·<u>jees</u>

taxi rank [BE] πιάτσα ταξί <u>piah</u>·tsah
tah·<u>ksee</u>

teaspoon κουταλάκι koo·tah·<u>lah</u>·kee

team n ομάδα oh·<u>mah</u>·THah

teenager έφηβος <u>eh</u>·fee·vohs

telephone n τηλέφωνο
tee·<u>leh</u>·foh·noh

telephone booth τηλεφωνικός
θάλαμος tee·leh·foh·nee·<u>kohs</u>
<u>thah</u>·lah·mohs

telephone call κλήση <u>klee</u>·see

telephone directory τηλεφωνικός
κατάλογος tee·leh·foh·nee·<u>kohs</u>
kah·<u>tah</u>·loh·ghohs

telephone number αριθμός

τηλεφώνου ah-reeth-<u>mohs</u>
tee-leh-<u>foh</u>-noo

tell λέω <u>leh</u>-oh

temperature (body) θερμοκρασία
theh-rmohk-rah-<u>see</u>-ah

temple ναός nah-<u>ohs</u>

temporary προσωρινός
proh-soh-ree-<u>nohs</u>

tennis τέννις <u>teh</u>-nees

tennis court γήπεδο τέννις
<u>yee</u>-peh-THoh <u>teh</u>-nees

tent σκηνή skee-<u>nee</u>

terrible φοβερός foh-veh-<u>rohs</u>

theater θέατρο <u>theh</u>-aht-roh

theft κλοπή kloh-<u>pee</u>

there εκεί eh-<u>kee</u>

thermal bath ιαματικό λουτρό
ee-ah-mah-tee-<u>koh</u> loot-roh

thermos flask θερμός thehr-<u>mohs</u>

thick χοντρός khohn-<u>drohs</u>

thief κλέφτης <u>klehf</u>-tees

thin *adj* **λεπτός** lehp-<u>tohs</u>

think νομίζω noh-<u>mee</u>-zoh

thirsty διψάω THee-<u>psah</u>-oh

those εκείνα eh-<u>kee</u>-nah

throat λαιμός leh-<u>mohs</u>

thumb αντίχειρας ahn-<u>dee</u>-khee-rahs

ticket εισιτήριο ee-see-<u>tee</u>-ree-oh

ticket office γραφείο εισιτηρίων
ghrah-<u>fee</u>-oh ee-see-tee-<u>ree</u>-ohn

tie *n* **γραβάτα** ghrah-<u>vah</u>-tah

tight *adj* **στενός** steh-<u>nohs</u>

tights [BE] *n* **καλσόν** kahl-<u>sohn</u>

timetable [BE] δρομολόγιο
THroh-moh-<u>loh</u>-yee-oh

tire λάστιχο lahs-tee-khoh

tired κουρασμένος
koo-rahz-<u>meh</u>-nohs

tissue χαρτομάντηλο
khahr-toh-<u>mahn</u>-dee-loh

toaster τοστιέρα toh-<u>stieh</u>-rah

tobacco καπνός kahp-<u>nohs</u>

tobacconist καπνοπωλείο
kahp-noh-poh-<u>lee</u>-oh

toilet [BE] τουαλέτα too-ah-<u>leh</u>-tah

toilet paper χαρτί υγείας khahr-<u>tee</u>
ee-<u>yee</u>-ahs

toiletries καλλυντικά
kah-leen-dee-<u>kah</u>

tongue γλώσσα <u>ghloh</u>-sah

too (extreme) πάρα πολύ <u>pah</u>-rah
poh-<u>lee</u>

tooth δόντι <u>THohn</u>-dee

toothache πονόδοντος
poh-<u>noh</u>-THohn-dohs

toothbrush οδοντόβουρτσα
oh-THohn-<u>doh</u>-voor-tsah

toothpaste οδοντόπαστα
oh-THohn-<u>doh</u>-pahs-tah

top *adj* **πάνω** <u>pah</u>-noh

torn σχισμένος skheez-<u>meh</u>-nohs

tour guide ξεναγός kseh-nah-<u>ghohs</u>

tourist τουρίστας too-<u>rees</u>-tahs

towards προς prohs

tower πύργος <u>peer</u>-ghohs

town πόλη <u>poh</u>-lee

town hall δημαρχείο
THee-mahr-<u>khee</u>-oh

γραφείο εισιτηρίων ghrah·<u>fee</u>·oh ee·see·tee·<u>ree</u>·ohn **ticket office**

γραφείο πληροφοριών ghrah·<u>fee</u>·oh plee·roh·foh·ree·<u>ohn</u> **information office**

γράφω <u>ghrah</u>·foh **write (down)**

γρήγορα <u>ghree</u>·ghoh·rah *adv* **fast**

γρήγορος <u>ghree</u>·ghoh·rohs **quick**

γρίππη <u>ghree</u>·pee **flu**

γυαλιά yah·<u>liah</u> **glasses (optical)**

γυαλιά ηλίου yah·<u>liah</u> ee·<u>lee</u>·oo **sun glasses**

γυναικολόγος yee·neh·koh·<u>loh</u>·ghohs **gynecologist**

γυρίζω yee·<u>ree</u>·zoh *v* **turn**

γωνία ghoh·<u>nee</u>·ah **corner**

Δ

δανείζω THah·<u>nee</u>·zoh **lend**

δάσος <u>THah</u>·sohs *n* **forest (wood)**

δάχτυλο <u>THakh</u>·tee·loh *n* **finger**

δείγμα <u>THeegh</u>·mah **specimen**

δείχνω <u>THeekh</u>·noh *v* **point (show)**

δέντρο <u>THehn</u>·droh **tree**

δεξιός THeh·ksee·<u>ohs</u> *adj* **right (not left)**

δέρμα <u>THehr</u>·mah *n* **skin**

δημαρχείο THee·mahr·<u>khee</u>·oh **town hall**

δημοφιλής THee·moh·fee·<u>lees</u> **popular**

δηλητήριο THee·lee·<u>tee</u>·ree·oh *n* **poison**

δηλητηριώδης

THee·lee·tee·<u>ree</u>·oh·THees **poisonous**

δηλώνω THee·<u>loh</u>·noh **declare**

δήλωση THee·loh·see **statement (legal)**

δημόσιος THee·<u>moh</u>·see·ohs **public**

διαμάντι THiah·<u>mahn</u>·dee *n* **diamond**

διαμέρισμα THee·ah·<u>meh</u>·reez·mah **apartment**

διάβαση πεζών THee·<u>ah</u>·vah·see peh·<u>zohn</u> **pedestrian crossing**

διαβατήριο THiah·vah·<u>tee</u>·ree·oh **passport**

διαβητικός THee·ah·vee·tee·<u>kohs</u> **diabetic**

διαδρομή THee·ahTH·roh·<u>mee</u> *n* **route**

διάδρομος THee·<u>ah</u>·THroh·mohs **aisle seat**

διαζευγμένος THee·ah·zehv·<u>ghmeh</u>·nohs **divorced**

διακοπές THee·ah·koh·<u>pehs</u> **vacation [holiday BE]**

διακόπτης THiah·<u>koh</u>·ptees *n* **switch**

διαμέρισμα THee·ah·mehr·ees·mah *n* **flat**

διάρροια THee·<u>ah</u>·ree·ah **diarrhea**

διάσημος THee·<u>ah</u>·see·mohs **famous**

διεθνής THee·eth·<u>nees</u> **international**

διεθνής φοιτητική κάρτα THee·ehth·<u>nees</u> fee·tee·tee·<u>kee</u> kahr·tah **International Student Card**

διερμηνέας THee·ehr·mee·<u>neh</u>·ahs

interpreter
διεύθυνση THee·<u>ehf</u>·theen·see *n*
  address
διευθυντής THee·ehf·theen·<u>dees</u>
  manager
δικηγόρος THee·kee·<u>ghoh</u>·rohs
  lawyer
δίκλινο δωμάτιο <u>THeek</u>·lee·noh
  THoh·<u>mah</u>·tee·oh **double room**
δίνω <u>THee</u>·noh **give**
διόρθωμα THee·<u>ohr</u>·thoh·mah *n* **trim**
δίπλα <u>THeep</u>·lah **next to**
διπλό κρεβάτι THeep·<u>loh</u> kreh·<u>vah</u>·tee
  twin bed
δίσκος <u>THees</u>·kohs **tray**
διψάω THee·<u>psah</u>·oh **thirsty**
δοκιμάζω THoh·kee·<u>mah</u>·zoh **try on**
δολάριο THoh·<u>lah</u>·ree·oh **dollar**
δόντι <u>THohn</u>·dee **tooth**
δοσολογία THoh·soh·loh·<u>yee</u>·ah
  dosage
δουλειά THoo·<u>liah</u> **job**
δουλεύω THoo·<u>leh</u>·voh **work**
δρομολόγιο THroh·moh·<u>loh</u>·yee·oh
  time table
δρόμος <u>THroh</u>·mohs **road, street,**
  way
δυνατός THee·nah·<u>tohs</u> *adj* **loud**
δυσάρεστος THee·<u>sah</u>·reh stohs
  unpleasant
δύσκολος <u>THees</u>·koh·lohs **difficult**
δυσπεψία THes·peh·<u>psee</u>·ah
  indigestion
δυστυχώς THees·tee·<u>khohs</u>

unfortunately
δυτικά <u>THee</u>·tee·<u>kah</u> **west**
δωμάτιο <u>THoh</u>·mah·tee·oh *n* **room**
δώρο <u>THoh</u>·roh **gift**

E

ελιά eh·liah **olive**
εμβόλιο ehm·<u>voh</u>·lee·oh **vaccination**
εμπορικό κέντρο ehm·boh·ree·<u>koh</u>
  <u>keh</u>·ntroh **shopping mall [centre**
  BE]
εγγύηση eh·<u>gee</u>·ee·see *n* **guarantee**
εγγυώμαι eh·gee·oh·meh *v*
  guarantee
έγκαυμα ηλίου <u>ehn</u>·gahv·mah
  ee·<u>lee</u>·oo *n* **sun burn**
έγκυος <u>eh</u>·gee·ohs **pregnant**
έδαφος <u>eh</u>·THah·fohs **ground (earth)**
εδώ eh·<u>THoh</u> **here**
εδώ κοντά eh·<u>THoh</u> kohn·<u>dah</u> **nearby**
εθνική οδός ehth·nee·<u>kee</u> oh·<u>THohs</u>
  highway, motorway
εθνικός eth·nee·<u>kohs</u> **national**
εθνικός δρυμός eth·nee·<u>kohs</u>
  THree·<u>mohs</u> **nature reserve**
είμαι <u>ee</u>·meh **be**
είμαι κουφός koo·<u>fohs</u> **deaf**
είδη οικιακής χρήσεως ee·<u>THee</u>
  ee·kee·ah·<u>kees</u> khree·seh·ohs
  household articles
ειδική ανάγκη ee·THee·<u>kee</u>
  ah·<u>nahn</u>·gkee **special requirement**
ειδικός ee·THee·<u>kohs</u> **specialist**
είδος <u>ee</u>·THohs **kind (sort)**

203

ζημιά zee·<u>miah</u> *n* **damage**
ζητώ zee·<u>toh</u> **ask**
ζωγραφίζω zohgh·rah·<u>fee</u>·zoh *v* **paint**
ζωγράφος zohgh·<u>rah</u>·fohs **painter**
ζώνη <u>zoh</u>·nee **belt**
ζώνη για χρήματα <u>zoh</u>·nee yah <u>khree</u>·mah·tah **money-belt**

Η

ημερομηνία λήξεως ee·meh·roh·mee·<u>nee</u>·ah <u>lee</u>·kseh·ohs **expiration date**
ημερολόγιο ee·meh·roh·<u>loh</u>·yee·oh **calendar**
ημικρανία ee·mee·krah·<u>nee</u>·ah **migraine**
ηλεκτρικός ee·lehk·tree·<u>kohs</u> **electric**
ηλεκτρονικό εισιτήριο ee·leh·ktroh·nee·<u>koh</u> ee·see·<u>tee</u>·ree·oh **e-ticket**
ηλεκτρονικό ταχυδρομείο (e-mail) ee·lehk·troh·nee·<u>koh</u> tah·hee·dro·<u>mee</u>·oh (ee·meh·eel)
ηλεκτροπληξία ee·leh·ktroh·plee·<u>ksee</u>·ah **shock (electric)**
ηλίαση ee·<u>lee</u>·ah·see **sun stroke**
ηλικιωμένος ee·lee·kee·oh·<u>meh</u>·nohs **senior citizen**
Ηνωμένες Πολιτείες ee·noh·<u>meh</u>·nehs poh·lee·<u>tee</u>·ehs **United Sstates**
Ηνωμένο Βασίλειο ee·noh·<u>meh</u>·noh vah·<u>see</u>·lee·oh **United Kingdom**
ηρεμιστικό ee·reh·mee·stee·<u>koh</u> **sedative**
ήσυχος <u>ee</u>·see·khohs *adj* **quiet**

Θ

θάλασσα <u>thah</u>·lah·sah **sea**
θέατρο <u>theh</u>·aht·roh **theater**
θέλω <u>theh</u>·loh **want**
θέρμανση <u>thehr</u>·mahn·see **heating**
θερμή πηγή thehr·<u>mee</u> pee·<u>yee</u> **hot spring**
θερμόμετρο thehr·<u>moh</u>·meht·roh **thermometer**
θερμοκρασία theh·rmohk·rah·<u>see</u>·ah **temperature (body)**
θερμός thehr·<u>mohs</u> **thermos flask**
θέρετρο διακοπών <u>theh</u>·reh·troh THee·ah·koh·<u>pohn</u> **vacation resort**
θέση <u>theh</u>·see *n* **location (space), seat**
θέση δίπλα στο παράθυρο <u>theh</u>·see THeep·lah stoh pah·<u>rah</u>·thee·roh **window seat**
θηλυκός thee·lee·<u>kohs</u> **female**
θορυβώδης thoh·ree·<u>voh</u>·THees **noisy**
θρησκεία three·<u>skee</u>·ah **religion**
θυμάμαι thee·<u>mah</u>·meh **remember**
θυρίδα thee·<u>ree</u>·THah **luggage locker (lock-up)**

Ι

ιατρική εξέταση ee·ah·tree·<u>kee</u>

eh-kseh-tah-see **examination (medical)**

ίδιος ee-THee-ohs **same**

ιδιωτικό μπάνιο ee-THee-oh-tee-koh bah-nioh **private bathroom**

ιερέας ee-eh-reh-ahs **priest**

ινσουλίνη een-soo-lee-nee **insulin**

ίντερνετ ee-nteh-rnet **internet**

ίντερνετ καφέ ee-nteh-rnet kah-feh **internet cafe**

ιπποδρομία ee-poh-THroh-mee-ah **horse racing**

ιστιοπλοϊκό ees-tee-oh-ploh-ee-koh **sailing boat**

ιστορία ee-stoh-ree-ah **history**

ισχύει ee-skhee-ee **valid**

ίσως ee-sohs **maybe, perhaps**

ιώδειο ee-oh-THee-oh **iodine**

K

κάδος απορριμμάτων kah-THohs ah-poh-ree-mah-tohn **trash can**

καθαρισμός προσώπου kah-thah-reez-mohs proh-soh-poo **facial**

καθαρός kah-thah-rohs **clean**

καθαρτικό kah-thahr-tee-koh **laxative**

καθεδρικός ναός kah-theh-THree-kohs nah-ohs **cathedral**

καθήκον kah-thee-kohn **duty (obligation)**

κάθομαι kah-thoh-meh **sit**

καθρέφτης kah-threhf-tees *n* **mirror**

καθυστέρηση kah-thee-steh-ree-see *n* **delay**

καθυστερώ kah-thee-steh-roh *v* **delay**

καινούργιος keh-noor-yohs **new**

καιρός keh-rohs **weather**

καλά kah-lah *adv* **fine (well)**

καλαμάκι kah-lah-mah-kee **straw (drinking)**

καλάθι kah-lah-THee **basket**

καλός kah-lohs **good**

καλσόν kahl-sohn *n* **tights**

κάλτσες kahl-tsehs **socks**

κάλυμμα φακού kah-lee-mah fah-koo **lens cap**

καλώ kah-loh *v* **call**

κάμπινγκ kah-mpeeng **camping**

καναπές kah-nah-pehs **sofa**

κανένας kah-neh-nahs *adj* **none**

κάνω ανάληψη kah-noh ah-nah-lee-psee **withdraw**

κάνω εμετό kah-noh eh-meh-toh *v* **vomit**

κάνω κράτηση kah-noh krah-tee-see *v* **book**

κάνω πεζοπορία kah-noh peh-zoh-poh-ree-ah *v* **hike**

καπέλο kah-peh-loh **hat**

καπνίζω kahp-nee-zoh *v* **smoke**

καπνοπωλείο kahp-noh-poh-lee-oh **tobacconist**

καπνός kahp-nohs **tobacco**

καραντίνα kah-rahn-dee-nah *n* **quarantine**

καράφα kah-rah-fah **carafe**

καρδιά kahr·THee·<u>ah</u> v **heart**

καρδιακό έμφραγμα kahr·THee·ah·<u>koh</u> <u>ehm</u>·frahgh·mah **heart attack**

καροτσάκι kah·roh·<u>tsah</u>·kee **trolley (cart)**

καροτσάκια αποσκευών kah·roh·<u>tsah</u>·kiah ah·pohs·keh·<u>vohn</u> **baggage [BE] carts [trolleys]**

κάρτα-κλειδί <u>kahr</u>·tah klee·<u>dee</u> **key card**

καρτποστάλ kahrt·poh·<u>stahl</u> **post card**

κασκόλ kahs·<u>kohl</u> **scarf**

κασσίτερος kah·<u>see</u>·teh·rohs **pewter**

κάστρο <u>kahs</u>·troh **castle**

καταδυτικός εξοπλισμός kah·tah·THee·tee·<u>kohs</u> eh·ksoh·pleez·<u>mohs</u> **diving equipment**

καταλαβαίνω kah·tah·lah·<u>veh</u>·noh **understand**

κατάλληλος kah·<u>tah</u>·lee·lohs **suitable**

καταρράχτης kah·tah·<u>rahkh</u>·tees **waterfall**

κατάστημα kah·<u>tah</u>·stee·mah **shop (store)**

κατάστημα με αντίκες kah·<u>tah</u>·stee·mah meh ahn·<u>tee</u>·kehs **antiques store**

κατάστημα με είδη δώρων kah·<u>tahs</u>·tee·mah meh <u>ee</u>·THee <u>THoh</u>·rohn **gift store**

κατάστημα με υγιεινές τροφές kah·<u>tahs</u>·tee·mah meh ee·yee·ee·<u>nehs</u> troh·<u>fehs</u> **health food store**

κατάστημα μεταχειρισμένων ειδών kah·<u>tah</u>·stee·mah meh·tah·khee·reez·<u>meh</u>·nohn ee·<u>THohn</u> **second-hand shop**

κατάστημα αθλητικών ειδών kah·<u>tahs</u>·tee·mah ath·lee·tee·<u>kohn</u> ee·<u>THohn</u> **sporting goods store**

κατάστημα ρούχων kah·<u>tahs</u>·tee·mah <u>roo</u>·khohn **clothing store**

κατάστημα σουβενίρ kah·<u>tahs</u>·tee·mah soo·veh·<u>neer</u> **souvenir store**

κατάστημα υποδημάτων kah·<u>tah</u>·stee·mah ee·poh·THee·<u>mah</u>·tohn **shoe store**

καταστρέφω kah·tah·<u>streh</u>·foh v **damage**

κατάψυξη kah·<u>tah</u>·psee·ksee **freezer**

κατεβαίνω kah·teh·<u>veh</u>·noh **get off (transport)**

κατειλημένος kah·tee·lee·<u>meh</u>·nohs **occupied**

κάτι <u>kah</u>·tee **something**

κάτοχος <u>kah</u>·toh·khohs **owner**

κατσαβίδι kah·tsah·<u>vee</u>·THee **screwdriver**

κατσαρόλα kah·tsah·<u>roh</u>·lah **saucepan**

κάτω <u>kah</u>·toh adj **lower (berth)**

καύσωνας kahf·soh·nahs **heat wave**
καφετέρια kah·feh·<u>teh</u>·ree·ah **cafe**
κέντρο της πόλης kehn·droh tees <u>poh</u>·lees **downtown area**
κεφάλι keh·<u>fah</u>·lee *n* **head**
κήπος <u>kee</u>·pohs *n* **garden**
κιθάρα kee·<u>thah</u>·rah **guitar**
κινηματογράφος kee·nee·mah·tohgh·<u>rah</u>·fohs **movie theater**
κίνηση <u>kee</u>·nee·see **traffic**
κινητό kee·nee·<u>toh</u> **cell phone [mobile phone BE]**
κίτρινος <u>keet</u>·ree·nohs **yellow**
κλειδαριά klee·THahr·<u>yah</u> *n* **lock (door)**
κλειδί klee·<u>THee</u> *n* **key**
κλειδώνω klee·<u>THoh</u>·noh *v* **lock (door)**
κλειστός klees·<u>tohs</u> *adj* **shut**
κλεμένος kleh·<u>meh</u>·nos **stolen**
κλέφτης <u>klehf</u>·tees **thief**
κλήση <u>klee</u>·see *n* **call**
κλιματισμός klee·mah·teez·<u>mohs</u> **air conditioning**
κλοπή kloh·<u>pee</u> **theft**
κομμωτήριο koh·moh·<u>tee</u>·ree·oh **hair dresser**
κόμβος <u>kohm</u>·vohs **junction (intersection)**
κοιμάμαι kee·<u>mah</u>·meh *v* **sleep**
κοιλάδα kee·<u>lah</u>·THah **valley**
κοιτάω kee·<u>tah</u>·oh *v* **look**
κολύμβηση koh·<u>leem</u>·vee·see **swimming**
κοντά kohn·<u>dah</u> *adv* **near**
κοντός kohn·<u>dohs</u> *adj* **short**
κορίτσι koh·<u>ree</u>·tsee **girl**
κορυφή koh·ree·<u>fee</u> *n* **peak**
κοσμηματοπωλείο kohz·mee·mah·toh·poh·<u>lee</u>·oh **jeweler**
κουβέρτα koo·<u>veh</u>·rtah **blanket**
κουζίνα koo·<u>zee</u>·nah **stove**
κουνούπι koo·<u>noo</u>·pee **mosquito**
κουρασμένος koo·rahz·<u>meh</u>·nohs **tired**
κουστούμι koos·<u>too</u>·mee **men's suit**
κουταλάκι koo·tah·<u>lah</u>·kee **teaspoon**
κουτάλι koo·<u>tah</u>·lee *n* **spoon**
κουτί koo·<u>tee</u> **carton**
κουτί πρώτων βοηθειών koo·<u>tee</u> proh·tohn voh·ee·thee·<u>ohn</u> **first-aid kit**
κράμπα <u>krahm</u>·bah *n* **cramp**
κραγιόν krah·<u>yohn</u> **lipstick**
κρατώ krah·<u>toh</u> *v* **keep**
κρέμα ξυρίσματος <u>kreh</u>·mah ksee·<u>reez</u>·mah·tohs **shaving cream**
κρεμάστρα kreh·<u>mahs</u>·trah **hanger**
κρεβάτι kreh·<u>vah</u>·tee **bed**
κρυολόγημα kree·oh·<u>loh</u>·yee·mah *n* **cold (flu)**
κρύος <u>kree</u>·ohs *adj* **cold (temperature)**
κρύσταλλο <u>kree</u>·stah·loh *n* **crystal**
κύμα <u>kee</u>·mah *n* **wave**
κυλικείο kee·lee·<u>kee</u>·oh **snack bar**
κυλιόμενες σκάλες

οφείλω oh‑<u>fee</u>‑loh **have to (obligation)**

οφθαλμίατρος ohf‑thahl‑<u>mee</u>‑aht‑rohs **optician**

Π

παγοπέδιλα pah‑ghoh‑<u>peh</u>‑THee‑lah **skates**

πάγος pah‑ghohs *n* **ice**

παιδική χαρά peh‑THee‑<u>kee</u> khah‑<u>rah</u> **playground**

παιδικό κρεβάτι peh‑THee‑<u>koh</u> kreh‑<u>vah</u>‑tee **crib [cot BE]**

παίζω <u>peh</u>‑zoh *v* **play (games, music)**

παιχνίδι pehkh‑nee‑THee *n* **game (toy), round**

παιχνίδι βίντεο pehkh‑<u>nee</u>‑THee <u>vee</u>‑deh‑oh **video game**

πακέτο pah‑<u>keh</u>‑toh **parcel**

πακέτο για το σπίτι pah‑<u>keh</u>‑toh yah toh <u>spee</u>‑tee **take away**

παλιά πόλη pah‑<u>liah</u> <u>poh</u>‑lee **old town**

παλιός pah‑<u>liohs</u> **old (thing)**

πάνα μωρού <u>pah</u>‑nah moh‑<u>roo</u> **diaper**

Πανεπιστήμιο pah‑neh‑pees‑<u>tee</u>‑mee‑oh **university**

πάνες μωρού <u>pah</u>‑nehs moh‑<u>roo</u> **nappies**

πανόραμα pah‑<u>noh</u>‑rah‑mah **panorama**

παντελόνι pahn‑deh‑<u>loh</u>‑nee **pants [trousers BE]**

παντοπωλείο pahn‑doh‑poh‑<u>lee</u>‑oh **minimart**

παντόφλες pahn‑<u>dohf</u>‑lehs **slippers**

παντρεμένος pahn‑dreh‑<u>meh</u>‑nohs **married**

πάνω <u>pah</u>‑noh *adj* **top, upper (berth)**

παπούτσι pah‑<u>poo</u>‑tsee **shoe**

πάρα πολύ <u>pah</u>‑rah poh‑<u>lee</u> **too (extreme)**

παραγγέλνω pah‑rah‑<u>gehl</u>‑noh *v* **order**

παράδειγμα pah‑<u>rah</u>‑THeegh‑mah **example**

παραδοσιακός pah‑rah‑THoh‑see‑ah‑<u>kohs</u> **traditional**

παράθυρο pah‑<u>rah</u>‑thee‑roh **window**

παραλαβή αποσκευών pah‑rah‑lah‑<u>vee</u> ah‑poh‑skeh‑<u>vohn</u> **baggage [BE] claim**

παραλία pah‑rah‑<u>lee</u>‑ah **beach**

παραλία γυμνιστών pah‑rah‑<u>lee</u>‑ah yeem‑nees‑<u>tohn</u> **nudist beach**

παραλυσία pah‑rah‑lee‑<u>see</u>‑ah **paralysis**

παράνομος pah‑<u>rah</u>‑noh‑mohs **illegal**

παράξενος pah‑<u>rah</u>‑kseh‑nohs **strange**

παραπάνω pah‑rah‑<u>pah</u>‑noh **more**

παρεξήγηση pah‑reh‑<u>ksee</u>‑yee‑see **misunderstanding**

πάρκο <u>pahr</u>‑koh *n* **park**

παρκόμετρο pahr‑<u>koh</u>‑meht‑roh **parking meter**

πάρτυ <u>pah</u>‑rtee *n* **party (social gathering)**

παυσίπονο pahf·see·poh·noh **painkiller**

παχύς pah·khees *adj* **fat (person)**

πέδιλα peh·THee·lah **sandals**

πεζόδρομος peh·zohTH·roh·mohs **pedestrian zone**

περιμένω peh·ree·meh·noh *v* **hold on, wait**

περιμένω στην ουρά peh·ree·meh·noh steen oo·rah *v* **queue [BE]**

περιέχω peh·ree·eh·khoh **contain**

περιοδικό peh·ree·oh·THee·koh **magazine**

περίοδος peh·ree·oh·THohs **period (menstrual)**

περιοχή peh·ree·oh·khee **region**

περιοχή για καπνίζοντες peh·ree·oh·khee yah kahp·nee·zohn·dehs **smoking area**

περιοχή για πικνίκ peh·ree·oh·khee yah peek neek **picnic area**

περίπτερο peh·ree·pteh·roh **newsstand, kiosk**

περνώ pehr·noh *v* **pass**

περπατώ pehr·pah·toh *v* **walk**

περσίδες peh·rsee·THehs **blinds**

πετάω peh·tah·oh *v* **fly**

πετσέτα peh·tseh·tah **napkin**

πέφτω pehf·toh *v* **fall**

πηγαίνω pee·yeh·noh **go**

πιάτσα ταξί piah·tsah tah·ksee **taxi rank [BE]**

πίεση pee·eh·see **blood pressure**

πιθανός pee·thah·nohs **possible**

πινακίδα pee·nah·kee·THah **road sign**

πίνω pee·noh *v* **drink**

πίπα pee·pah **pipe (smoking)**

πιπίλα pee·pee·lah **pacifier [soother BE]**

πισίνα pee·see·nah **swimming pool**

πιστοποιητικό ασφάλειας pees·toh·pee·ee·tee·koh ahs·fah·lee·ahs **insurance certificate**

πιστωτική κάρτα pees·toh·tee·kee kahr·tah **credit card**

πιτσαρία pee·tsah·ree·ah **pizzeria**

πλαγιά plah·yah **slope (ski)**

πλαστική σακούλα plahs·tee·kee sah·koo·lah **plastic bag**

πλατίνα plah·tee·nah **platinum**

πλευρό plehv·roh **rib**

πλημμύρα plee·mee·rah *n* **flood**

πληγή plee·yee **wound (cut)**

πληροφορίες plee·roh·foh·ree·ehs **information**

πληρωμή plee·roh·mee **payment**

πληρώνω plee·roh·noh *v* **pay**

πλοίο plee·oh *n* **ship**

πλυντήριο pleen·deer·ee·oh **washing machine**

πνεύμονας pnehv·moh·nahs **lung**

πόμολο poh·moh·loh *n* **handle**

ποδήλατο poh·THee·lah·toh **bicycle**

πόδι poh·THee **foot, leg**

ποδόσφαιρο poh·THohs·feh·roh **soccer [football BE]**

ποιότητα pee·**oh**·tee·tah **quality**

πόλη **poh**·lee **town**

πολυκατάστημα
poh·lee·kah·**tahs**·tee·mah
department store

πολυτέλεια poh·lee·**teh**·lee·ah **luxury**

πολύτιμος poh·**lee**·tee·mohs
valuable

πονόδοντος poh·**noh**·THohn·dohs
toothache

πονοκέφαλος poh·noh·**keh**·fah·lohs
headache

πονόλαιμος poh·**noh**·leh·mohs **sore throat**

πόνος **poh**·nohs n **pain**

πόνος στο αυτί **poh**·nohs stoh ahf·**tee**
earache

πόρτα **pohr**·tah **door**

πορτοφόλι pohr·toh·**foh**·lee **wallet**

ποσό poh·**soh** n **amount**

ποσότητα poh·**soh**·tee·tah **quantity**

ποταμός poh·tah·**mohs** **river**

ποτέ poh·**teh** **never**

ποτήρι poh·**tee**·ree **glass (container)**

ποτό poh·**toh** n **drink**

πουκάμισο poo·**kah**·mee·soh **shirt**

πράσινος **prah**·see·nohs **green**

πρέπει **preh**·pee v **must**

πρεσβεία prehz·**vee**·ah **embassy**

πρεσβύωπας prehz·**vee**·oh·pahs
long-sighted [BE]

πρήξιμο **pree**·ksee·moh **swelling**

πρησμένος preez·**meh**·nohs **swollen**

πρίζα **pree**·zah n **plug, socket**

πριν preen **before**

πρόβλεψη **prohv**·leh·psee n **forecast**

πρόβλεψη καιρού **prohv**·leh·psee
keh·**roo** **weather forecast**

πρόβλημα **prohv**·lee·mah **problem**

πρόγραμμα **prohgh**·rah·mah n
program

πρόγραμμα θεαμάτων proh·ghrah·
mah theh·ah·**mah**·tohn **program
of events**

προς prohs **towards**

προσαρμοστής proh·sahr·moh·**stees**
adaptor

πρόσβαση **prohz**·vah·see n **access**

προσγειώνομαι
prohz·yee·**oh**·noh·meh v **land**

προσκαλώ prohs·kah·**loh** v **invite**

πρόσκληση **prohs**·klee·see **invitation**

πρόστιμο **prohs**·tee·moh n **fine
(penalty)**

πρόσωπο **proh**·soh·poh n **face**

προσωρινός proh·soh·ree·**nohs**
temporary

προτείνω proh·**tee**·noh **suggest**

προφέρω proh·**feh**·roh **pronounce**

προφυλακτικό proh·fee·lah·
ktee·**koh** **condom**

προωθώ proh·oh·**thoh** **forward**

πρωί proh·**ee** **morning**

πρωινό proh·ee·**noh** **breakfast**

πρώτη θέση **proh**·tee theh·see **first
class**

πτήση **ptee**·see **flight**

πυρετός pee·reh·**tohs** **fever**

πυροσβεστήρας pee·rohz·vehs·tee·rahs **fire extinguisher**

πυροσβεστική pee·rohz·vehs·tee·kee **fire brigade [BE]**

πυτζάμες pee·jah·mehs **pajamas**

Ρ

ραδιόφωνο rah·THee·oh·foh·noh *n* **radio**

ρακέτα rah·keh·tah **racket (tennis, squash)**

ραντεβού rahn·deh·voo **appointment**

ράφι rah·fee *n* **shelf**

ρεματιά reh·mah·tiah **ravine**

ρεσεψιόν reh·seh·psiohn **reception (hotel)**

ρεύμα ποταμού rehv·mah poh·tah·moo **rapids**

ρηχή πισίνα ree·khee pee·see·nah **paddling pool**

ρομαντικός roh·mahn·dee·kohs **romantic**

ρολόι roh·loh·ee *n* **watch**

ρυάκι ree·ah·kee *n* **stream**

Σ

σμαράγδι zmah·rahgh·THee **emerald**

σαμπουάν sahm·poo·ahn *n* **shampoo**

σαγιονάρες sah·yoh·nah·rehs **flip-flops**

σαγόνι sah·ghoh·nee **jaw**

σάκκος sah·kohs **knapsack**

σαλόνι sah·loh·nee **living room**

σάουνα sah·oo·nah **sauna**

σαπούνι sah·poo·nee *n* **soap**

σατέν sah·tehn **satin**

σβήνω svee·noh *v* **turn off**

σβώλος svoh·lohs *n* **lump**

σεζ-λονγκ sehz lohng **deck chair**

σενιάν seh·niahn **rare (steak)**

σερβιέτες sehr·vee·eh·tehs **sanitary towels**

σεσουάρ seh·soo·ahr **hair dryer**

σήμα see·mah **sign (road)**

σημαία see·meh·ah *n* **flag**

σημαίνω see·meh·noh *v* **mean**

σημείο see·mee·oh *n* **point**

σίδερο see·THeh·roh *n* **iron**

σιδερώνω see·THeh·roh·noh *v* **iron, press**

σιδηροδρομικός σταθμός see·THee·rohTH·roh·mee·kohs stahth·mohs **rail station**

σκάλα skah·lah **ladder**

σκάλες skah·lehs **stairs**

σκηνή skee·nee **tent**

σκι skee **skiing**

σκιά skee·ah **shade (darkness)**

σκοπός skoh·pohs **purpose**

σκούπα skoo·pah *n* **broom**

σκουπίδια skoo·peeTH·yah **trash [rubbish BE]**

σκούρος skoo·rohs *adj* **dark (color)**

σλιπ sleep **briefs**

σόλα soh·lah **sole (shoes)**

σορτς sohrts *n* **shorts**

σουβενίρ soo·veh·neer **souvenir**

σουπερμάρκετ soo·pehr·<u>mahr</u>·keht **supermarket**

σουτιέν soo·<u>tiehn</u> **bra**

σπα spah **spa**

σπάγγος <u>spah</u>·gohs *n* **string (cord)**

σπάνιος <u>spah</u>·nee·ohs **rare (unusual)**

σπασμένος spahz·<u>meh</u>·nohs **broken**

σπάω <u>spah</u>·oh *v* **break**

σπήλαιο <u>spee</u>·leh·oh *n* **cave**

σπίρτο <u>speer</u>·toh *n* **match (to start fire)**

σπονδυλική στήλη spohn·THee·lee·<u>kee</u> <u>stee</u>·lee **spine**

σπουδάζω spoo·<u>THah</u>·zoh *v* **study**

σταματώ stah·mah·<u>toh</u> *v* **stop**

στάδιο <u>stah</u>·THee·oh **stadium**

σταθμός μετρό stahth·<u>mohs</u> meh·<u>troh</u> **subway [underground BE] station**

σταθμός λεωφορείων stahTH·<u>mohs</u> leh·oh·foh·<u>ree</u>·ohn **bus station**

στάση <u>stah</u>·see **exposure (photos), stop (bus)**

στάση λεωφορείου <u>stah</u>·see leh·oh·foh·<u>ree</u>·oo **bus stop**

στέγη <u>steh</u>·yee *n* **roof**

στέλνω <u>stehl</u>·noh **send**

στενός steh·<u>nohs</u> *adj* **narrow, tight**

στήθος <u>stee</u>·THohs **breast**

στόμα <u>stoh</u>·mah *n* **mouth**

στομάχι stoh·<u>mah</u>·khee *n* **stomach**

στομαχόπονος stoh·mah·<u>khoh</u>·poh·nohs **stomach ache**

στολή stoh·<u>lee</u> *n* **uniform**

στολή δύτη stoh·<u>lee</u> <u>THee</u>·tee **wetsuit**

στρογγυλός strohn·gkee·<u>lohs</u> *adj* **round**

στυλ steel *n* **style**

στυλό stee·<u>loh</u> *n* **pen**

συμπεριλαμβάνεται seem·beh·ree·lahm·<u>vah</u>·neh·teh **included**

σύζυγος <u>see</u>·zee·ghohs **husband, wife**

συκώτι see·<u>koh</u>·tee **liver**

σύμπτωμα <u>seem</u>·ptoh·mah **symptom**

συναγερμός πυρκαγιάς see·nah·yehr·<u>mohs</u> peer·kah·<u>yahs</u> **fire alarm**

συναντώ see·nahn·<u>doh</u> **meet**

συνέδριο see·<u>neh</u>·THree·oh **conference**

συνταγή γιατρού seen·dah·<u>yee</u> yaht·<u>roo</u> **prescription**

συνταγογραφώ seen·dah·ghoh·ghrah·<u>foh</u> **prescribe**

συνταξιούχος seen·dah·ksee·<u>oo</u>·khohs **retired**

σύντομα <u>seen</u>·doh·mah **soon**

συντριβάνι seen·dree·<u>vah</u>·nee **fountain**

συστάσεις see·<u>stah</u>·sees **introductions**

συστήνω see·<u>stee</u>·noh **introduce, recommend**

συχνός seekh·<u>nohs</u> *adj* **frequent**

σφηνωμένος sfee·noh·<u>meh</u>·nohs **jammed**

σφράγισμα sfrah·yeez·mah **filling (dental)**

σφυρί sfee·<u>ree</u> **hammer**

σχέδιο skheh·THee·oh *n* **plan**

σχήμα skhee·mah *n* **shape**

σχισμένος skheez·<u>meh</u>·nohs **torn**

σχοινί skhee·<u>nee</u> *n* **rope**

σχολή σκι skhoh·<u>lee</u> skee **ski school**

σωσίβιο soh·<u>see</u>·vee·oh **lifejacket**

σωστός sohs·<u>stohs</u> *adj* **right (correct)**

T

ταμπόν tahm·<u>bohn</u> **tampon**

τάβλι <u>tah</u>·vlee **backgammon**

ταγιέρ tah·<u>yehr</u> **women's suit**

ταΐζω tah·<u>ee</u>·zoh *v* **feed**

ταινία teh·<u>nee</u>·ah **movie**

ταξί tah·<u>ksee</u> **taxi**

ταξίδι tah·<u>ksee</u>·THee **journey**

ταξίδι με πλοίο tah·<u>ksee</u>·THee meh <u>plee</u>·oh **boat trip**

ταξιδιωτική επιταγή tah·ksee·<u>THee</u>·oh·tee·<u>kee</u> eh·pee·tah·<u>yee</u> **traveler's check [traveller's cheque BE]**

ταξιδιωτικό γραφείο tah·ksee·<u>THyoh</u>·tee·<u>koh</u> ghrah·<u>fee</u>·oh **travel agency**

ταξιτζής tah·ksee·<u>jees</u> **taxi driver**

ταυτότητα tahf·<u>toh</u>·tee·tah **identification**

ταχυδρομείο tah·kheeTH·roh·<u>mee</u>·oh **post office**

ταχυδρομική επιταγή tah·kheeTH·roh· mee·<u>kee</u> eh·pee·tah·<u>yee</u> **money order**

ταχυδρομικό κουτί tah·kheeTH·roh·mee·<u>koh</u> koo·<u>tee</u> **mailbox [postbox BE]**

τεμάχιο teh·<u>mah</u>·khee·oh **piece**

τελειώνω teh·lee·<u>oh</u>·noh *v* **end**

τελευταίος teh·lehf·<u>teh</u>·ohs **last**

τελεφερίκ teh·leh·feh·<u>reek</u> **cablecar**

τέλος <u>teh</u>·lohs *n* **end**

τελωνειακή δήλωση teh·loh·nee·ah·<u>kee</u> THee·loh·see **customs declaration (tolls)**

τελωνείο teh·loh·<u>nee</u>·oh **customs (tolls)**

τέννις <u>teh</u>·nees **tennis**

τετράγωνος teht·<u>rah</u>·ghoh·nohs **square**

τζετ-σκι jeht skee **jet-ski**

τζόγκιγκ joh·geeng **jogging**

τζόγος <u>joh</u>·ghohs **gambling**

τηλεκάρτα tee·leh·<u>kahr</u>·tah **phone card**

τηλεόραση tee·leh·<u>oh</u>·rah·see **TV**

τηλεφώνημα tee·leh·<u>foh</u>·nee·mah **phone call**

τηλεφωνικός θάλαμος tee·leh·foh·nee·<u>kohs</u> <u>thah</u>·lah·mohs **telephone booth**

τηλεφωνικός κατάλογος tee·leh·foh·nee·<u>kohs</u> kah·<u>tah</u>·loh·ghohs **telephone directory**

τηλέφωνο tee·<u>leh</u>·foh·noh *n* **phone**

την teen **per**

τιμή συναλλάγματος tee·mee see·nah·<u>lahgh</u>·mah·tohs **exchange rate**

τιμή εισόδου tee·<u>mee</u> ee·<u>soh</u>·THoo **entrance fee**

τιρμπουσόν teer·boo·<u>sohn</u> **corkscrew**

τοίχος tee·khohs **wall**

τοπικός toh·pee·<u>kohs</u> **local**

τοστιέρα toh·<u>stieh</u>·rah **toaster**

τουαλέτα too·ah·<u>leh</u>·tah **restroom [toilet BE]**

τούνελ <u>too</u>·nehl **tunnel**

τουρίστας too·<u>rees</u>·tahs **tourist**

τουριστική θέση too·ree·stee·<u>kee</u> <u>theh</u>·see **economy class**

τουριστικός οδηγός too·ree·stee·<u>kohs</u> oh·THee·<u>ghohs</u> **guide book**

τραβώ το καζανάκι trah·<u>voh</u> toh kah·zah·<u>nah</u>·kee **flush**

τραμ trahm **tram**

τράπεζα trah·peh·zah **bank**

τραπέζι trah·<u>peh</u>·zee **table**

τραπεζομάντηλο trah·peh·zoh·<u>mahn</u>·dee·loh **tablecloth**

τραυματισμένος trahv·mah·teez·<u>meh</u>·nohs **injured**

τρένο <u>treh</u>·noh **train**

τρέχω <u>treh</u>·khoh *v* **run, speed**

τρόμπα <u>troh</u>·mbah *n* **pump**

τρόλλεϋ <u>troh</u>·leh·ee **trolley-bus**

τρύπα <u>tree</u>·pah **hole (in clothes)**

τρώω <u>troh</u>·oh **eat**

τσάντα <u>tsahn</u>·dah **handbag**

τσίμπημα <u>tsee</u>·bee·mah *n* **bite, sting (insect)**

τσίμπημα κουνουπιού <u>tseem</u>·bee·mah koo·noo·<u>piooh</u> **mosquito bite**

τυπικός tee·pee·<u>kohs</u> **typical**

τύχη <u>tee</u>·khee **luck**

Υ

υγρό πιάτων eegh·<u>roh</u> <u>piah</u>·tohn **dishwashing detergent**

υπεραστικό λεωφορείο ee·peh·rahs·tee·<u>koh</u> leh·oh·foh·<u>ree</u>·oh **long-distance bus**

υπεραστικό τηλεφώνημα ee·pehr·ahs·tee·<u>koh</u> tee·leh·<u>foh</u>·nee·mah **long-distance call**

υπέρβαρο ee·<u>pehr</u>·vah·roh **excess baggage [BE]**

υπηκοότητα ee·pee·koh·<u>oh</u>·tee·tah **nationality**

υπηρεσία ee·pee·reh·<u>see</u>·ah *n* **service (administration, business)**

υπηρεσία δωματίου ee·pee·reh·<u>see</u>·ah THoh·mah·<u>tee</u>·oo **room service**

υπηρεσία πλυντηρίου ee·pee·reh·<u>see</u>·ah pleen·dee·<u>ree</u>·oo **laundry service**

υπνόσακκος ee-<u>pnoh</u>-sah-kohs **sleeping bag**

υπνωτικό χάπι eep-noh-tee-<u>koh</u> <u>khah</u>-pee **sleeping pill**

υπόγειος ee-<u>poh</u>-ghee-ohs **underground [BE]**

υπολογιστής ee-poh-loh-yee-<u>stees</u> **computer**

υπόνομος ee-<u>poh</u>-noh-mohs **sewer**

ύφασμα <u>ee</u>-fahs-mah **fabric (cloth)**

ύψος <u>ee</u>-psohs **height**

Φ

φακός fah-<u>kohs</u> **flashlight, lens**

φακός επαφής fah-<u>kohs</u> eh-pah-<u>fees</u> **contact lens**

υπηρεσία φαξ ee-pee-reh-<u>see</u>-ah fahks **fax facility**

φάρμα <u>fahr</u>-mah n **farm**

φάρμακα <u>fahr</u>-mah-kah **medication**

φαρδύς fahr-<u>THees</u> **loose (fitting), wide**

φάρος <u>fah</u>-rohs **lighthouse**

φέρνω <u>fehr</u>-noh **bring**

φέρυ-μπωτ <u>feh</u>-ree boht **ferry**

φεστιβάλ fehs-tee-<u>vahl</u> **festival**

φεύγω <u>fehv</u>-ghoh v **leave (depart)**

φιλμ feelm n **film (camera)**

φίλη <u>fee</u>-lee **girlfriend**

φιλί fee-<u>lee</u> n **kiss**

φιλοδώρημα fee-loh-<u>THoh</u>-ree-mah **gratuity**

φίλος <u>fee</u>-lohs **friend, boyfriend**

φίλτρο <u>feel</u>-troh n **filter**

φιλώ fee-<u>loh</u> v **kiss**

φλέβα <u>fleh</u>-vah **vein**

φλεγμονή flegh-moh-<u>nee</u> **inflammation**

φλυτζάνι flee-<u>jah</u>-nee **cup**

φοβερός foh-veh-<u>rohs</u> **terrible**

φοβισμένος foh-veez-<u>meh</u>-nohs **frightened**

φοιτητής fee-tee-<u>tees</u> **student**

φόρεμα <u>foh</u>-reh-mah n **dress**

φόρος <u>foh</u>-rohs **duty (customs), tax**

φορώ foh-<u>roh</u> v **wear**

φούρνος <u>foor</u>-nohs **oven**

φούρνος μικροκυμάτων <u>foor</u>-nohs mee-kroh-kee-<u>mah</u>-tohn **microwave (oven)**

φούστα <u>foo</u>-stah **skirt**

φούτερ <u>foo</u>-tehr **sweatshirt**

ΦΠΑ fee-pee-<u>ah</u> **sales tax**

φράγμα <u>frahgh</u>-mah n **lock (river, canal)**

φράση <u>frah</u>-see n **phrase**

φράχτης <u>frahkh</u>-tees n **fence**

φρέσκος <u>frehs</u>-kohs adj **fresh**

φτάνω <u>ftah</u>-noh **arrive**

φτηνός ftee-<u>nohs</u> **cheap, inexpensive**

φτιάχνω τις βαλίτσες ftee-<u>ahkh</u>-noh tees vah-<u>lee</u>-tsehs v **pack (baggage)**

φυλακή fee-lah-<u>kee</u> n **prison**

φύση <u>fee</u>-see **nature**

φυτό fee-<u>toh</u> n **plant**

φως fohs n **light (electric)**

φώτα <u>foh</u>-tah **lights (car)**

φωτογραφία foh·tohgh·rah·<u>fee</u>·ah v **photo**

φωτογραφική μηχανή foh·tohgh·rah·fee·<u>kee</u> mee·khah·<u>nee</u> **camera**

φωτοτυπικό foh·toh·tee·pee·<u>koh</u> **photocopier**

Χ

χαμηλώνω khah·mee·<u>loh</u>·noh v **turn down** (volume, heat)

χαλί khah·<u>lee</u> **rug**

χαλκός khahl·<u>kohs</u> **copper**

χάπι <u>khah</u>·pee **tablet**

χάρτης <u>khahr</u>·tees n **map**

χαρτί khar·<u>tee</u> **paper**

χαρτί κουζίνας khah·<u>rtee</u> koo·<u>zee</u>·nahs **kitchen**

χαρτί υγείας khahr·<u>tee</u> ee·<u>yee</u>·ahs **toilet paper**

χαρτομάντηλο khahr·toh·<u>mahn</u>·dee·loh **tissue**

χαρτομάντηλο khah·rtoh·<u>mahn</u>·dee·loh **handkerchief**

χείλη <u>khee</u>·lee **lips**

χειροκίνητος khee·roh·<u>kee</u>·nee·tohs **manual** (car)

χειρότερος khee·<u>roh</u>·teh·rohs **worse**

χιλιόμετρα khee·<u>lioh</u>·meh·trah **mileage**

χιονίζει khioh·<u>nee</u>·zee v **snow**

χλιαρός khlee·ah·<u>rohs</u> **lukewarm**

χόμπυ <u>khoh</u>·bee **hobby** (pastime)

χοντρός khohn·<u>drohs</u> **thick**

χορεύω khoh·<u>reh</u>·voh v **dance**

χορτοφάγος khohr·toh·<u>fah</u>·ghohs **vegetarian**

χρειάζομαι khree·<u>ah</u>·zoh·meh v **need**

χρέωση υπηρεσίας <u>khreh</u>·oh·see ee·pee·reh·<u>see</u>·ahs **service charge**

χρήματα <u>khree</u>·mah·tah **money**

χρησιμοποιώ khree·see·moh·pee·<u>oh</u> v **use**

χρήσιμος <u>khree</u>·see·mohs **useful**

χρονική περίοδος khroh·nee·<u>kee</u> peh·<u>ree</u>·oh·THohs **period** (time)

χρυσός khree·<u>sohs</u> n **gold**

χρώμα <u>khroh</u>·mah n **color**

χρωστώ khroh·<u>stoh</u> **owe**

χτένα <u>khteh</u>·nah n **comb**

χτενίζω khteh·<u>nee</u>·zoh v **comb**

χτες khtehs **yesterday**

χώρα <u>khoh</u>·rah **country** (nation)

χωριό khohr·<u>yoh</u> **village**

χωρίς khoh·<u>rees</u> **without**

χώρος <u>khoh</u>·rohs n **space** (area)

χώρος κάμπινγκ <u>kah</u>·mpeeng <u>khoh</u>·rohs **campsite**

χώρος στάθμευσης <u>khoh</u>·rohs <u>stahth</u>·mehf·sees **car park** [BE]

χώρος στάθμευσης <u>khoh</u>·rohs <u>stahth</u>·mehf·sees **parking lot**

Ψ

ψαλίδι psah·<u>lee</u>·THee **scissors**

ψάρεμα <u>psah</u>·reh·mah **fishing**

ψάχνω <u>psahkh</u>·noh **look for**

Berlitz®

speaking your language

phrase book & dictionary
phrase book & CD

Available in: Arabic, Cantonese Chinese, Croatian, Czech, Danish, Dutch, English*, Finnish*, French, German, Greek, Hebrew*, Hindi, Hungarian*, Indonesian, Italian, Japanese, Korean, Latin American Spanish, Mandarin Chinese, Mexican Spanish, Norwegian, Polish, Portuguese, Romanian*, Russian, Spanish, Swedish, Thai, Turkish, Vietnamese

*Book only

www.berlitzpublishing.com

ψηλός psee·<u>lohs</u> **tall**
ψύλλος <u>psee</u>·lohs **flea**

Ω

ώμος <u>oh</u>·mohs *n* **shoulder (anatomy)**
ώρα αιχμής <u>oh</u>·rah ehkh·<u>mees</u> **rush
  hour**
ώρες λειτουργίας <u>oh</u>·rehs
  lee·toor·<u>yee</u>·ahs **opening hours**